PENGUIN BOOKS

THE NEW PENGUIN FREUD
GENERAL EDITOR: ADAM PHILLIPS

The Unconscious

Sigmund Freud was born in 1856 in Moravia; between the ages of
four and eighty-two his home was in Vienna: in 1938 Hitler's invasion
of Austria forced him to seek asylum in London, where he died in
the following year. His career began with several years of brilliant
work on the anatomy and physiology of the nervous system. He was
almost thirty when, after a period of study under Charcot in Paris,
his interests first turned to psychology; and after ten years of clinical
work in Vienna (at first in collaboration with Breuer, an older col-
league) he invented what was to become psychoanalysis. This began
simply as a method of treating neurotic patients through talking, but
it quickly grew into an accumulation of knowledge about the workings
of the mind in general. Freud was thus able to demonstrate the
development of the sexual instinct in childhood and, largely on
the basis of an examination of dreams, arrived at his fundamental
discovery of the unconscious forces that influence our everyday
thoughts and actions. Freud's life was uneventful, but his ideas
have shaped not only many specialist disciplines, but also the whole
intellectual climate of the twentieth century.

Graham Frankland was born in 1969. He has published one book
about Freud, his doctoral thesis *Freud's Literary Culture* (Cambridge
University Press, 2000), and he is currently writing a second one,
Language and Its Discontents, supported by a Leverhulme Special
Research Fellowship. He lectures in German at the University of
Liverpool.

Mark Cousins was educated at Oxford University and the Warburg
Institute. He is currently Director of General Studies and Head of
the Histories and Theories graduate programme at the Architectural
Association.

Adam Phillips was formerly Principal Child Psychotherapist at Charing Cross Hospital in London. He is the author of several books on psychoanalysis including *On Kissing, Tickling and Being Bored. Darwin's Worms, Promises, Promises* and *Houdini's Box*.

SIGMUND FREUD

The Unconscious

Translated by Graham Frankland
with an Introduction by Mark Cousins

PENGUIN BOOKS

PENGUIN BOOKS

Penguin Books Ltd, 80 Strand, London WC2R ORL, England
Penguin Group (USA) Inc., 375 Hudson Street, New York, New York 10014, USA
Penguin Group (Canada), 10 Alcorn Avenue, Toronto, Ontario, Canada M4V 3B2
(a division of Pearson Penguin Canada Inc.)
Penguin Ireland, 25 St Stephen's Green, Dublin 2, Ireland
(a division of Penguin Books Ltd)
Penguin Group (Australia), 250 Camberwell Road, Camberwell, Victoria 3124, Australia
(a division of Pearson Australia Group Pty Ltd)
Penguin Books India Pvt Ltd, 11 Community Centre, Panchsheel Park, New Delhi – 110 017, India
Penguin Group (NZ), cnr Airborne and Rosedale Roads, Albany, Auckland 1310, New Zealand
(a division of Pearson New Zealand Ltd)
Penguin Books (South Africa) (Pty) Ltd, 24 Sturdee Avenue, Rosebank 2196, South Africa

Penguin Books Ltd, Registered Offices: 80 Strand, London WC2R ORL, England

www.penguin.com

Formulierungen über die zwei Prinzipien des psychischen Geschehens first
published 1911 in *Jahrbuch für psychoanalytische und psychopathologische
Forschungen* 3 (1)
Triebe und Triebschicksale first published 1915 in *Internationale Zeitschrift für
ärtzliche Psychoanalyse* 3 (2)
Die Verdrängung first published 1915 in *Internationale Zeitschrift für ärtzliche
Psychoanalyse* 3 (3)
Das Unbewußte first published 1915 in *Internationale Zeitschrift für ärtzliche
Psychoanalyse* 3 (4)
Die Verneinung first published 1925 in *Imago* 11 (3)
Fetischismus first published 1927 in *Almanach 1928*
Die Ichspaltung im Abwehrvorgang first published (posthumously) 1940 in
Internationale Zeitschrift für Psychoanalyse und Imago 25 (3–4)
This translation published in Penguin Classics 2005

030

Sigmund Freud's German texts collected in *Gesammelte Werke* (1940–52)
copyright © Imago Publishing Co., Ltd, London, 1941, 1943, 1946, 1948
Translation and editorial matter copyright © Graham Frankland, 2005
Introduction copyright © Mark Cousins, 2005
All rights reserved

Set in 10/12.5 pt PostScript Adobe New Caledonia
Typeset by Rowland Phototypesetting Ltd, Bury St Edmunds, Suffolk
Printed and bound in Great Britain by Clays Ltd, Elcograf S.p.A.

ISBN-13: 978-0-141-18388-6

www.greenpenguin.co.uk

Contents

Introduction

The ratio between clarity and obscurity at the level of knowledge tipped towards obscurity in the nineteenth century. Problem after scholarly problem withdrew from a field of transparent relations into opacity. What was said, what was done, what was expressed no longer belonged to a human discourse illuminated by reason and understood by spontaneous consciousness. Suddenly the thought of demonstrating a universal truth by referring to an inner certainty was becoming buffoonish, a quack philosophy. Everything was becoming less self-evident including the self. The subject was surrounded not by a transparent world but by overlapping systems which did not disclose their conditions of intelligibility. For Michel Foucault in *The Order of Things*, the domains of language, life and labour each became obscure objects whose real nature was not only different, but at variance with the way in which they appeared to human consciousness. The system of language, whether considered as a grammatical structure or as the condensation of a culture, was not available to a speaker. Even as the subject seemed to speak the language, it was the language which spoke the subject. In an emergent biology, the subject lived and died in a process whose mechanisms completely escaped him. And in society the subject laboured to reproduce a system that was not his intent, over which he had no control, and whose workings were hidden from subjective life.

It is not surprising, then, that the nineteenth century needed a strong idea of the unconscious to depict the relations of the subject to the objects of his reality, and to the question of knowledge. Individual disciplines emerged precisely to bring back those objects into the field of public knowledge. The specifically modern sense of 'disciplines' was proposed to rectify the general problem of 'obscurity'. What the subject now lacked in the ruins of common sense could be provided by disciplined knowledges. The subject could be educated. But this education, thought to stem from a new type of university and a new model of science and new models of the dissemination of knowledge, needed a general language to communicate the results and the significance of that knowledge. It found it in the category of interpretation, in the practice of linking the positive knowledges to what was taken as their 'meaning' in a broad sense. Public discourse used as its primary currency the question of the consequences, the potentiality, the historical meaning of the new disciplines – of linguistics, of biology, of political economy. Public discourse worked along the axis of the unconscious and interpretation. The subject who lacked a conscious grasp of phenomena was to be restored by an education in knowledge, whose significance was the work of interpretation.

Given this, it is not surprising that many historians of ideas have insisted that Freud's work was deeply embedded in the nineteenth century. The two terms 'unconscious' and 'interpretation' are sufficient signs of this. The presumption that the subject does not have conscious, spontaneous access to what determines him, that a knowledge is a disciplined interpretation of material, theoretically established and justified by evidence – all this is indeed a position which Freud shared with orthodox intellectual culture of the nineteenth century. And Freud never lost these convictions nor the hope that psychoanalysis would take its place among the human sciences. Much of what historians say in asserting that Freud was at home in the nineteenth century is true. Indeed, where else would he be at home? But amongst other things Freud warned against the category of 'at home'. Home is more than it seems to be.

The papers collected in this volume, if they did nothing else, would sharply distinguish Freud's concept of the unconscious from his nineteenth-century precursors. Sometimes, for literary reasons, as in the opening passages of the paper *The Unconscious*, he aligns himself with a certain orthodoxy by repeating a critique of consciousness. Consciousness is full of 'gaps'. It simply does not function as a continuous and exhaustive representation of what we know. We forget things, we make slips of the tongue, and above all we hold most thoughts, feelings and knowledge in a realm of latency. From this we must infer that the mind at the least is made up of at least two registers – consciousness and the realm of latency. This is true, but was perfectly conventional. It in no way expresses the radicalism to which Freud puts the idea of the unconscious. Or rather it is only one of three senses of the unconscious that he himself comes to deploy and that these papers argue for. Freud's theory of the unconscious, even while it shared affinities with nineteenth-century thought, is the space in which he inserted something so radically different that it not only did not inhabit the nineteenth century, it was never really accommodated by the twentieth century. These papers constitute the vivid and central scene of Freud's thought on this question.

And yet before approaching them, two qualifications have to be entered. Despite the argument mounted here concerning the centrality of these papers, they are not amongst the most frequently cited works of Freud. Perhaps they do not make the textual appeal of the case studies or *The Interpretation of Dreams*; nor do they elicit the fascination, whether querulous or credulous, of *Totem and Taboo* or *Moses and Monotheism*. They do not project the Olympian point of view of *Civilization and Its Discontents*. They do not provide an overall account of the subject, of the psychical apparatus as a whole. They do not start from the realities of psychoanalytical practice. They do not charm and disarm the reader by being that worldly cicerone who guides his imaginary audience through the field of psychoanalysis as in the various series of lectures. Compared with all these attractions within the work of Freud, these papers have seemed too many to be dry, unrelieved exercises in a kind of psychoanalytic logic – the formulation of propositions and their abstract revision by means of qualification or supplement. Often these papers have been charged with being examples of Freud's dogmatism. Even for those who have granted Freud's acuity, these papers are amongst those which show that beyond the force of Freud's thought there lurked an intransigent dogmatism, a layer of axioms justified neither by science nor a grasp of the human heart.

Nor are these papers perhaps the most dramatic statements of his views of the unconscious. Of course the fact is that almost the whole of Freud's writings might be treated as his contribution to a theory of the unconscious. Most obviously in *The Interpretation of Dreams*, Freud tried to establish how dreams constituted a privileged layer of evidence not only of unconscious and unfulfilled wishes but of evidence of the unconscious as such. It also dealt with the separation from and the form of connection of the unconscious with the rest of the psychical apparatus. Chapter 7 of that work serves as an indispensable statement of Freud's position on the unconscious that is still his position during the composition of the papers in this volume. But by then a number of tensions had appeared in the theory of the unconscious which would force Freud to revise his position. Other accounts both brief and elaborate can be found in other works of Freud.

All this is a long way round to the question of the significance of these particular papers within Freud's works. In the view of this reader they are central and invaluable for a reason which perhaps at first is not entirely evident. It is true that they present in a coherent manner Freud's general view of the unconscious, but they are not alone in Freud's work in doing this. They stress again that for Freud the unconscious was more then something missing from consciousness. In the paper *The Unconscious* Freud relegates this sense to what he calls the descriptive unconscious. But the descriptive unconscious is for Freud merely the beginning of an exploration of the psyche. He makes a further distinction between the preconscious and the unconscious which corresponds to the distinction between psychic material which is merely latent and psychic material which is made unconscious by the act of repression. There is now a certain landscape of the psyche opened up in which fields of consciousness, the preconscious and the unconscious are distinguished from each other, with the agent of repression lying on the border of the preconscious and the unconscious. This image of psychical regions of course in no way corresponds with any anatomical locations. It is a differentiated landscape, what Freud calls a topographical sense of the psyche. He adds to this a description of the energy and its circulation through the psyche, which he calls the economic definition of the unconscious. What this energy is lies at the heart of Freud's conception of the unconscious. The energy draws upon instinctual life, but is not confined by the concept of instinct, which always invokes the simple mechanism of stimulus and response. This transformed energy arises on the borders between the biological and the psychical, and Freud develops various formulations to account for what occurs on this boundary. It continues to remain an uncertain area of Freud's theory, but one thing is certain – once within the psychical system the energy becomes what the current translator rightly translates as the 'drives'. What any plausible account of the boundary must include is, on the one hand, the way instinctual energy becomes bound into psychic life and, on the other hand, how that binding into the psychic life of the individual can still be understood in terms of intensity. For it is certainly Freud's conviction that this psychical energy can be expressed in terms of relative quantities and that indeed this constitutes another register of the unconscious, the economic. This completes the triad of the descriptive, the topographical and the economic. The knitting together of all these three registers constitutes for Freud a metapsychological description of the psyche. Such a description will provide an account of how these registers cooperate or conflict in expressing the obedience of the psyche to what Freud calls the pleasure principle. This principle states that the entire psychical mechanism seeks pleasure but defines pleasure not in a hedonistic fashion but rather as the expulsion of excitation.

These points constitute a dry description of the unconscious. They represent simply the core of Freud's convictions about the unconscious during this period. They still give little idea of the character of these papers. One way of trying to get closer to the papers is to read them as being a kind of work in progress. They aren't expressed dogmatically except in the sense that Freud passes quickly over that which is currently no longer or not yet a problem, but in fact each of the papers focuses on major problems which themselves arise from the core concept of the unconscious. Far from charting Freud's dogmatism, they are efforts to deal with the consequences and contradictions of his theory, to work through them and to amend the theory as he went along. Once the papers are seen almost as the site of private theoretical work, their centrality can more easily be understood. This is Freud not in the mode of persuading or teaching or warning. This is a workplace, and the bluntness of the points made are in the service of his own self-clarification rather than an attempt to cajole the reader into acceptance.

It is enough here to detail some of the difficulties and problems that Freud opened up to see the way in which Freud worked when he was trying to *think* psychoanalysis rather than practice it. In the first paper of this collection, *Formulation on the Two Principles of Mental Functioning*, Freud raised the question of the relationship between the pleasure principle and reality. In pursuit of pleasure the subject meets the problem of reality. If the infant was unable to secure a feed in the real world, according to Freud the infant would hallucinate, but while hallucination can supply many things, it cannot produce milk. The infant reacts to this frustration by investigating the source of his non-satisfaction and by adding to his explanation of what is pleasurable an explanation of what is real. It appeared that wishes could profit from the investigation of reality. A knowledge of reality and a willingness to compromise with it seemed to provide the subject with a possible if shaky basis for development. Certainly Freud thought this could be a spur to curiosity and knowledge. But Freud's account of the relations between psychical reality and external reality lacked any instrumental optimism. Firstly, because of the nature of the pleasure principle. To talk about the *satisfaction* of wishes under its regime is exaggerated. The pleasure principle offers the temporary removal of a wish but within an economy of ultimate non-satisfaction. The wish arises again and again and again. Homeostasis is not satisfaction. But there is another sense in which Freud limited the psyche's capacity to benefit from the reality principle. Repressed psychical material cannot be drawn towards the reality principle; it is not even conscious. It turns away from reality. Freud does not give up his sense of a fundamental antagonism between the pleasure principle and the reality principle.

What is interesting is that, without noticing it, Freud makes here a contribution to the very idea of 'reality'. We might think that most philosophers would assert that 'reality' is whatever is the case; the human sciences might adjust that by thinking that 'reality' is all that people think is the case. Freud's concern to think out the difference between phantasy and reality leads him to the novel proposal that reality is an obstacle. It follows that the boundary between reality and phantasy is no longer something like the difference between a mental event and a real event. I am always within a phantasy as long as I meet no obstacle to its satisfaction. Reality is not a topographical category, it is not that which is outside my skin, it is whatever is an obstacle to the satisfaction of a wish. One way of charting the progress of Freud's thought is that he finds the obstacles of reality more and more efficacious in the block they offer to desire just as he becomes increasingly convinced by the archaic character of desire and its relative ineducability by reason and the world. The very existence of the unconscious had alienated the subject from his own consciousness. Now the unconscious alienates the subject from full acceptance of external reality. Ultimately the subject is the very battleground over which reality and phantasy lay their claims. Whatever the course of the struggle, it is weighted in favour of phantasy. Or, in Freud's terms, hate is older than love. This formula expresses the primary narcissism of the subject's very rejection of the stimuli of the outside world.

Such a view has important consequences for the elaboration of the concept of the drive. Certainly we cannot think simply of an object in reality, through which the subject attaches himself to the drive, even if situations may seem to conform to this formula. The drive can only find expression when it has been mediated by the elements of the psyche. Beyond its differentiation from the action of an instinct Freud needed to elaborate the idea of the drive so that it could function as an account of energy and as an element of the psyche, that is, as having some task of representation. In some sense this is one of the most acute problems with Freud's idea of the unconscious.

Drives and Their Fates is an attempt to elaborate the concept of drive so that it can be the mechanism through which what he had called phantasy could be made active. At one level the drive is that energy which originates within the organism and which what Freud calls the 'nervous system' exists to eliminate. Freud does not want to use the word 'stimulus' since it is too redolent of biology. At first he calls it a 'need'. But whether you call it a need, an object or even a stimulus, what is at stake is that the object of the drive is simply that through which the drive is able to achieve its aim. It is clear that for Freud the drive and its organization come first logically. The object is not importantly defined as an object; it is whatever 'fits' the drive. This idea in Freud ties in with what has already been said about the economic. It is vital for Freud's theory of the unconscious that it has this economic level. It also links with Freud's more psychological sense of an object, and the subject's choice of an object – that objects are all substitutes for a previous object, that to find an object is to re-find an object. The substitutive role of the object is another way of stating the economic priority of the drive.

This would seem to be a central idea in Freud and inevitably linked to the idea of the unconscious being expressed in economic terms. Yet it is an aspect of the theory which has attracted not only rejection from outside psychoanalysis but also within it. Since Freud, the biological understanding of instincts and the psychological understanding of mental processes have both moved away from the Freudian account of the drive. In this situation Freud's theory of the drive will often seem to orthodox psychology, neuropsychology, and cognitive theories of mental processes to be quite lacking in experimental validity and evidence. From this point of view, Freud is often regarded as a speculative precursor of an age in which a combination of genetics, theories of computation, and evolution, together with a mild dose of analytic philosophy, will finally uncover the secrets of the unconscious. Within psychoanalysis it is more the idea of the economic dimension and its relation to the drive that has come in for criticism or simply neglect.

Faced with the inexorable progress of measurement within psychology there has been an increasing reluctance to refer to a quantitative dimension within psychical life without being able to assign numbers or measured relations to it. The idea of forces and of relative strengths which yet could not produce a scale, smacked, to many, of a pre-scientific frame of mind. Yet as Freud saw clearly, the drive was inevitably a quantitative issue if his account of the unconscious was to have any meaning. Nor is it clear why one cannot speak of relative strengths outside the imposition of a scale. But it is also clear that another powerful objection to the economic dimension of the unconscious came about through a gradual post-Freudian sense of the object. In Freud's view and from the point of view of the pleasure principle the object is that which will satisfy the drive and will enable the accumulating excitation be discharged. The object has to be such that it will 'fit' the needs of the drives but is logically subordinate to the drive itself. Put in more psychological terms, it means that Freud's theory carries a certain emotional brutality. Certainly in Freud's terms the libido may invest itself in the object and may bind itself to the object. But if the object changes, or if the character of the drive changes, then the object becomes economically redundant and the drive will have to look for a substitute. This may seem a rather blatant formula, with few concessions to contemporary sentimentality, but it has the plain virtue of underlining Freud's axiom that the object is always already a substitute. Partly what is at stake here is the changing meaning of the word 'object'. Fairbain once asserted that man was '*an object seeking animal*'. A great deal hangs on this formulation and its influence. For it seems to transform a Freudian theory of the object of the drive into one in which the pleasure principle has been silently modified into a theory of intersubjective relations. Even what the term 'object' refers to seems to have altered. Instead of using the term 'object' as simply whatever would satisfy the drive, now the word seems to be surrounded by the aura of a human person. This indeed may be the aim of many therapeutic theories, but it is not Freud's. Freud's idea of the unconscious is one whose mechanisms are subordinate to the drives. For Freud, this is a reason for the interior of the psyche to match what he has already observed in respect to external reality – the unconscious is permanently locked into its own priority, its stony indifference to anything outside its own satisfaction. This also bears on the history of the subject. For Freud to find an object is always to re-find an object. The relation between subject and object is always a second-hand relation. The unconscious is a bargain hunter for whom the cost of living is always too high. On this account we cannot think of the object of the drive as another subject, though it may be represented by another subject. The object is better thought of as a phantasy, a set of enduring relations which will enable satisfaction of the subject's own configuration.

This is why Freud recognizes that the drive itself is always already complex. If the subject of the drive is the unconscious, and if we differentiate between the object and the aim of the drive, it is clear that the drive can undergo many modifications in the progress towards its discharge. This is why the issues of sadism/masochism and exhibitionism/voyeurism have such a strong representation in Freud's working out of the idea of the drives. He is not concerned with these conditions from a clinical or a case-historical point of view. He is concerned with them from the point of view of the *form*, and from the logic of how they can be transformed. Both can be viewed from the issue of the *reversal* of the drive, a reversal of the aim. And they can also be viewed from the issue of the reversal of the object, in which masochism becomes the shift of the object of one's sadism to one's own body. Reversing the aim and reversing the object are only two of the number of ways the drive can sustain itself within the regime of the pleasure principle. The point about sadism/masochism and voyeurism/exhibitionism is that Freud main-tains them as topics within discussions of the drive to keep a check on how complicated was becoming the join between them and the pleasure principle. Since Freud openly avowed that the very idea of the unconscious was an inference, and that of course no one could observe it, it followed, at least for Freud, that the theory ought to be simple or else it would lose its logical authority.

It should be clear by now that the papers on the unconscious, far from being dogmatic and assertive, are a continuous attempt by

Freud to move from the core of his certainty about the nature of the unconscious and the drives to the margins of his argument where he remained in doubt and in a state of continuous revision. The problem for Freud was that he knew that the theory of the unconscious had all to fit together, and so he found himself continuously working on those elements which did not fit or did not fit everything or no longer fitted if something else changed. Ultimately the theory began to show wear, to develop cracks and finally to require an entirely new footing for the theory of the unconscious and of the drives in what Freud called the second topography. These papers then also represent an increasingly awkward task for Freud to fulfill. The trouble perhaps sprang from the mechanism of the pleasure principle, that mechanism which brought together the question of the object, of the drive and of repression.

Obviously the pleasure principle was never exactly a hedonistic manifesto. Indeed one could be forgiven for wondering why it used the term 'pleasure'. What is at stake in the pleasure principle is the assumption that the human subject prefers to be in a state of homeostasis. To this end its task is always to expel excitement. The 'satisfaction' of wishes is merely an intermediate stage amongst the rhythms of homeostatic life. If the pleasure principle is supposed to explain all satisfactions of the drive then the problem was that the explanations had to become more and more complicated. This was the difficulty that Freud faced in the years of these papers. Sadism, exhibitionism and, above all, love were interrogated for the degree to which their most improbable results could still be looped back into the mechanism of the pleasure principle. One of those problems was the relation of the pleasure principle to wishing itself. For the principle seemed not only to harbour the means of dealing with wishes but also to oppose wishing. Several times a day I lose my glasses and my pen and I experience an intense wish to find them. So powerful is this wish that it seems to produce at its heart the temporary belief that if I found them, everything in my world would be alright. Then I find them and not everything in my world is alright. It is as if borne along on the wings of one wish to find my glasses or my pen is another wish – the wish to stop wishing. It is as though the impulse to homeostasis propels us to a sleepy disillusion with desire.

Everything in Freud's theory depends on the radical separation of consciousness and the unconscious. As Freud recognized, this requires an account of how something is removed from the sphere of consciousness and kept away from it. This is the task of repression. But these papers show a great deal of equivocation on Freud's part about the nature of repression. The immediate task of repression is precisely to keep unconscious drives away from conscious representation. But this does not account for whence repression comes, and Freud is forced to use a concept of primal repression. Repressed material continues to act and through reorganizations still seeks to gain satisfaction. Deprived of satisfaction the repression may lead to the formation of neurotic symptoms, in which case the repressed material is still kept away from conscious knowledge. Freud's account of repression remains unresolved through these papers and a source of continuing theoretical problems. This introduction has been concerned to suggest the importance of these papers and that, far from some dry exercise in psychoanalytic logic, they constitute a remarkable series of notes. Clearly, Freud was someone who thought through writing. One can suspect from these papers that he only noticed certain problems when they had been written down.

Freud is universally agreed to have been influential, but what does that mean? Such vague praise seems rather to express doubts about Freud's theory of the unconscious. A history of the acceptance and the rejection of his theory would surely show that while almost everybody accepted the descriptive sense of the unconscious there were few who would justify the economic sense of the unconscious. Whilst everyone might make a gestural acceptance of the unconscious, at the most general level there are probably relatively few who would wish to support all these papers. Freud would not have been surprised and would have had a Freudian reason to explain the lack of acceptance of his theory. The doctrine of the unconscious in his view completed a dethronement of Man started by Copernicus continued by Darwin and completed by Freud. Man was no longer at the centre of the universe, was no longer the highest form of creation, and now with the theory of the unconscious was no longer master in his own house. Freud took seriously the idea that his theory of the unconscious was such a blow to frail human narcissism that his theory would be rejected overwhelmingly by the forces of infantile life. It is this possibility which frequently enrages anti-Freudians. They feel that having raised the question of the truth or falsity of the theory of the unconscious, rather than being replied to they find their arguments reduced to the expression of their underlying emotion. But of course if this is unsettling it ought to at least be remembered that Freud's argument must also be applied to those who accept his theory. No one should be left in a comfortable position.

To the critic who rejects Freud's concept of the unconscious, there are various arguments which can be employed to support the rejection; one strong line of argument is that Freud avoids the norms and procedures of scientific observation or method. Certainly orthodox psychology has not in general welcomed the idea of the unconscious; nor has philosophy itself. While there is acceptance of the descriptive unconscious or what Freud called preconscious, this does not extend to embracing either a topographical, still less an economic, account of the unconscious or of the very idea of the primary process. This view often tends to the restrictive sense that while ideas and feelings may be unconscious, the term should always be thought of in an adjectival sense. To make a noun of it, to elevate it to a thing is to convert the true fact that not all contents of the mind are present to consciousness into the dogma of a mechanism. Philosophers of science might add that Freud's conviction in the existence of the unconscious does not allow of any falsification, and so evidence can neither confirm nor reject its resistance. To those who accept these criticisms the issue is clear: Freud was wrong.

But the situation is more complicated. For someone who accepts Freud's arguments, the above rejections might well betray an unconscious psychological motive. If it is perfectly clear that to a Freudian the rejection of the unconscious can be made to appear as a wounded *amour-propre*, in turn this is unlikely to satisfy the opponents for whom this form of reasoning itself is for them a strong reason to reject Freud. Nor is this the place to try to resolve the issue. It is enough to suggest that it is merely an extreme case of the failure of argument to persuade, let alone change anyone. Yet this is where psychoanalysis came in. It was founded in the moment of ceasing to 'attend' to the argument and starting to listen to it.

Translator's Preface

In his book *The Question of Lay Analysis* Freud writes of the psychoanalytical terms *Ich* and *Es*: 'You will probably protest at our having chosen simple pronouns to describe our two agencies or provinces instead of giving them orotund Greek names. In psychoanalysis, however, we like to keep in contact with the popular mode of thinking and prefer to make its concepts scientifically serviceable rather than to reject them.' He goes on to explain 'our theories must be understood by our patients, who are often very intelligent, but not always learned'. These comments take us to the heart of some of the key problems associated with translating Freud into English. Despite his forceful argument here, the English *Standard Edition of the Complete Psychological Works of Sigmund Freud* (24 vols., 1953–75), produced under the aegis of James Strachey, translates these 'simple pronouns' – literally, 'I' and 'it' – as 'ego' and 'id', and there can be little doubt that these remote, Latinate renderings of what are eminently plain, everyday German words represent a significant distortion of Freud's style.

Like many others who thoroughly enjoy the experience of reading Freud in the original German, I often found myself disappointed by the English translations in the *Standard Edition*, which frequently dissipate the simple lucidity and vivid force of Freud's prose. Penguin's project to retranslate key works of his was therefore instantly appealing. In attempting my own translations, I found that much improvement was to be had simply from translating Freud into more modern English, something rather less verbose than Strachey's English. This is often more a matter of syntax than of vocabulary as such. For example, I have frequently favoured simple verbal constructions where Strachey tends towards a more 'nominal' style, with long strings of nouns that can be slightly ponderous to the English ear.

Other more technical improvements are more or less a matter of consensus among Germanists interested in Freud. Most agree, for example, that the key psychoanalytical term *Trieb* is better translated simply by its English cognate 'drive' than by 'instinct'. Of course, such an elementary approach was not always possible. Indeed, my own greatest departure from it lies precisely in my translating the terms *Ich* and *Es* as 'ego' and 'id'. For better or worse, these Latin terms have now irretrievably passed into standard modern English – not least by dint of Freud's own enormous impact on twentieth-century consciousness. Generally, though, I have tried to bear in mind Freud's own declared preference for straightforward language, summarized in his 'Dora' case history with the words: 'J'appelle un chat un chat.' To give just a few examples: where for *Tasten* (Freud's metaphor for the thought process) Strachey has 'palpating', I have 'feeling out'; where for *Triebverschränkung* Strachey has 'confluence of instincts', I have 'overlapping drives'; and where Strachey has 'scopophilia', I have 'voyeurism' – a term as instantly comprehensible to an ordinary English speaker as *Schaulust* is to a German.

Of course, Freud's German has merits far beyond plain simplicity. What primarily attracted me to Penguin's project was their suggestion that the new translations be aimed at a non-specialist or 'literary' readership. I myself recently published a book entitled *Freud's Literary Culture* (CUP, 2000), which seeks to re-evaluate Freud as an inheritor of and contributor to literary traditions, and in it I specifically address the literary qualities of Freud's writing, qualities that are, to some extent, effaced by Strachey's attempt to homogenize Freud's prose into a more standard scientific register. Consequently, another guiding principle of my translations was to retain as much as possible of the rich allusiveness and imagery of Freud's German. The word *Besetzung*, for example, is laden with concrete meanings for a German speaker in a way that Strachey's 'cathexis' can never be for an English speaker. My own translation is 'investment' (or 'investment of energy', depending on the context), although 'charge' is, admittedly, an equally strong contender, and one that has the additional merit of resonating with the 'electricity' imagery so fundamental to Freud's metapsychology. In the end, however, I found 'investment' more immediately meaningful to a lay English reader and, more crucially, less ambiguous – indeed, I was already using the term 'emotive charge' to translate Freud's *Affektbetrag* ('quota of affect' in the *Standard Edition*).

More significantly – not least because it necessitated the total reworking of one of the essay titles – I have translated *Triebschicksale* as 'drive fates' (or, more frequently, 'the fates of drives', English being rather less free with such compounds than German). The *Standard Edition* rendering, 'instinctual vicissitudes', blithely disregards the fact that the word *Schicksal* is laced with connotations for Freud, a writer whose classical erudition – evident in his fascination with Oedipus, Narcissus, Eros, Thanatos, and so on – contributed so substantially towards making psychoanalysis something far richer and stranger than any quasi-Newtonian 'mechanics' of mental processes. Freud himself frequently writes about the literary concept of 'fate' in classical tragedy and about the Greek Fates themselves in his analyses of dreams and myths. Strachey's 'vicissitude' is such a gratuitous distortion that one cannot help suspecting it belongs to a more general attempt to remove the trace of some of the more humanistic sources of Freudian theory, the better to assert its putative scientific status.

As 'instinctual vicissitudes' aptly demonstrates, Strachey often shows rather too strong a preference for the polysyllabic, frequently compromising the vibrant yet easy – almost spoken – rhythm of Freud's prose. It was this consideration that prompted me, for example, to translate *psychisch* as 'psychic' rather than 'psychical', even if this meant trusting the intelligence of the reader to deduce from the context that 'psychic' here means nothing more mystical than 'pertaining to the psyche'. Similarly, I have preferred 'slip' to Strachey's 'parapraxis'. While it is true that Freud's *Fehlleistung* is a rather more complex and ambiguous term (hence some of the more outlandish alternatives suggested by would-be translators, for example Bruno Bettelheim's 'mischievement'), the word is nevertheless instantly comprehensible to any German speaker, and much of its post-Freudian complexity and ambiguity now attaches to the word 'slip' itself, so thoroughly has popular consciousness been permeated by the notion of the 'Freudian slip'. Of course, I have not made terseness – or any other of my basic criteria – into any kind of strict rule. There is no place for such inflexibility when weaving the delicate fabric of compromises that constitutes a sensitive translation. Thus, for example, my initial impulse may have been to translate *topisch* as 'topical' but, since *Topik* really has to be translated as 'topography', I happily reverted to the 'topographical' familiar from the *Standard Edition*. Indeed, another of my criteria – that of straightforward comprehensibility to a lay English reader – already gave 'topographical' the slight edge over the, potentially ambiguous, 'topical'.

My emphasis on plain, modern English – a notion that would, of course, collapse if one were to try to define it – is certainly not invulnerable to criticism. There are at least two instances in which certain readers are sure to be aggrieved by the licence I have derived from it. First, I have translated *Affekt* as 'emotion' rather than the more obvious – and semantically incontestable – 'affect', my overriding consideration being not semantic correctness but everyday contemporary usage. Similarly, to render *Vorstellung* I have used the term with the widest common currency – 'idea' – rather than the more philosophically correct 'presentation'. It should be borne in mind here that Freud himself was deeply suspicious of academic philosophy, and I cannot imagine he would have used the term *Vorstellung* quite so freely were it not also perfectly familiar to every German speaker as a standard word for 'idea'. Using the term 'presentation' – unfamiliar in this context to anyone without a philosophical background – would have made the relevant passages (where the word is heavily repeated, often in combinations such as *Wortvorstellung* and *Dingvorstellung*) rebarbative in a way that Freud strove consciously to avoid. (Incidentally, where it would not have been clear from the context that 'idea' here means the concrete content of an act of ideation, and not any kind of verbally formulated conception, I have translated *Vorstellung* as 'mental image'.)

❖

It is worth mentioning that the metapsychological essays that form the centrepiece of the present volume are perhaps especially problematic for the translator. Not only is Freud, as was his wont, evidently 'thinking with his pen' in these essays, they are further complicated by the state of violent flux in which psychoanalytical theory found itself just as Freud was attempting to formulate this grand – and ultimately abortive – summary of psychoanalytical theory. In fact, he was mired in one of his most intractable theoretical crises – the one initially provoked by his postulation of narcissism – whose ultimate outcome was his theory of the 'death drive'. This latter concept was soon to supersede, for example, Freud's attempt in 'Drives and their Fates' to account for the phenomenon of hate, and I would certainly ask any reader who finds my translation of this account occasionally rather tortuous to compare it with the German original before laying the blame entirely at the translator's door. I have, for example, always resisted taking the liberty – frequently arrogated by Strachey – of typographically rearranging Freud's texts. My own translations remain faithful to Freud's original paragraphing, parentheses, textual emphases, and so on, even where my first impulse was to clarify and 'tidy up' the original.

Of course, many of the difficulties of these essays simply add to their fascination as historical records of a great mind stretching itself to the limits. They were certainly not enough to discourage me in my belief that Strachey's translations could be improved upon. I should add, however, that the experience of translating Freud quickly taught me a new respect for the *Standard Edition*, not least on account of the sheer magnitude of the task undertaken by Strachey et al. My critical attitude towards their translations became ever more subdued as it was increasingly brought home to me just what a chimera the notion of an 'ideal' Freud translation is. Naturally I produced my own translations before referring back, for purposes of comparison, to the *Standard Edition*, and, although I have focused in this Preface on some of the more glaring differences, I should also add that I was equally struck by the great number of similarities that remained, even where I had agonized over multiple alternatives. This may simply reflect the extent to which Strachey's version of

Freud has entered our consciousness but, of course, it also indicates that, no matter how hard we new translators try, we are latecomers with a strong predecessor. Strachey has repeatedly beaten us to the best formulation. Having said this, I must add that these similarities were most uncanny in my translation of the paper 'Negation', which I suspect is due to the fact that, for this paper, Strachey simply revised a translation already made by the excellent Joan Riviere, who had no hidden agenda of providing Freud's works with some kind of extra scientific weight. I should count myself more than satisfied if my own translations were deemed to bear comparison with hers.

Finally, I should like to say a warm word of thanks to Dr Jim Simpson for his knowledgeable, sensitive and detailed critiques of my translations. I took the vast majority of his excellent suggestions on board, and it goes without saying that all remaining infelicities and errors are entirely my own.

Graham Frankland, 2001

Formulations on the Two Principles of Psychic Functioning

We have long observed that every neurosis has the effect, and so probably the purpose, of forcing the patient out of real life, of alienating him from reality. Such a fact could not escape Pierre Janet's attention; he spoke of a loss '*de la fonction du réel*' as a specific characteristic of neurotics, although without uncovering the connection between this dysfunction and the basic conditions of neurosis.[1]

We have gained some insight into this connection by introducing the process of repression into the aetiology of neurosis. The neurotic turns away from reality because he finds either the whole or parts of it unbearable. The most extreme type of this turning away from reality is exhibited in certain cases of hallucinatory psychosis where the patient attempts to deny the event that has triggered his insanity (Griesinger). Actually, though, every neurotic does the same thing with some fragment of reality.[2] Thus we are presented with the task of studying the development of the relationship of neurotics – and mankind in general – to reality, and so of assimilating the psychological significance of the real outside world into the framework of our theories.

We psychologists grounded in psychoanalysis have become accustomed to taking as our starting-point unconscious psychic processes, the peculiarities of which we have come to know through analysis. We consider these to be the older, primary psychic processes, remnants of a phase of development in which they were the only kind. The highest tendency obeyed by these primary processes is easy to identify; we call it the pleasure-unpleasure principle (or the pleasure principle for short). These processes strive to gain pleasure;

our psychic activity draws back from any action that might arouse unpleasure (repression). Our dreams at night, our tendency when awake to recoil from painful impressions, these are vestiges of the rule of this principle and evidence of its power.

I am relying on trains of thought developed elsewhere (in the general section of *The Interpretation of Dreams*) when I postulate that the state of equilibrium in the psyche was originally disrupted by the urgent demands of inner needs. At this stage, whatever was thought of (wished for) was simply hallucinated, as still happens every night with our dream-thoughts.[3] It was due only to the failure of the anticipated satisfaction, the disillusionment as it were, that this attempt at satisfaction by means of hallucination was abandoned. Instead, the psychic apparatus had to resolve to form an idea of the real circumstances in the outside world and to endeavour actually to change them. With this, a new principle of psychic activity was initiated; now ideas were formed no longer of what was pleasant, but of what was real, even if this happened to be unpleasant.[4] This inception of the *reality principle* proved to be a momentous step.

1) First, the new demands necessitated a series of adjustments in the psychic apparatus, which, due to our insufficient or uncertain knowledge, we can deal with only in passing here.

The increased significance of external reality heightened in turn the significance of the sense organs directed towards that outside world, and also of the *consciousness* attached to these, which now learnt how to discern sensory qualities in addition to the qualities of pleasure and unpleasure, previously its only concern. A specific function of *attention* was set up with the task of periodically scanning the outside world in order to assimilate its data in advance, should an urgent inner need arise. This activity seeks out sensory impressions rather than waiting for them to occur. Probably at the same time, a system of *retention* was set up with the task of storing the results of this periodic activity of consciousness, an element of what we call *memory*.

In place of repression, which excluded certain of the emerging ideas – those deemed unpleasurable – from being invested with energy, there arose a process of impartial *judgement*, whose task it was to decide if a particular idea was true or false – that is, corresponded with reality or not – a decision reached via comparisons made with memory traces of reality.

Motor discharge, which under the rule of the pleasure principle had served to relieve the psychic apparatus from increases in stimulation by means of innervations sent inside the body (physical gestures, expressions of emotion), was now given a new function, being deployed to make expedient alterations to external reality. It was transformed into *action*.

It now became necessary to hold motor discharge (action) in check, and this was achieved via the *thought process*, which evolved from basic ideation. Thought became endowed with qualities that enabled the psychic apparatus to tolerate the increase in tension from stimuli while discharge was deferred. A thought process is essentially a trial run of an action, displacing smaller quantities of invested energy and involving a low expenditure (discharge) of these. For this purpose, freely displaceable investments of energy had to be converted into fixed ones, which was achieved by raising the level of the whole process of energy investment. Thought – in so far as it went beyond simple ideation and dealt with the relations between object-impressions – was probably originally unconscious and did not acquire qualities perceptible to consciousness until it became linked to the memory traces of words.

2) A general tendency of our psychic apparatus, which can be traced back to the economic principle of conserving expenditure, seems to manifest itself in the tenacity with which we cling to existing sources of pleasure and the difficulty we have in giving these up. At the inception of the reality principle, one kind of thought activity split away, remaining exempt from reality-testing and continuing to obey only the pleasure principle.[5] This is *fantasizing*, which begins with children's play then later, as *daydreaming*, ceases to rely on actual objects.

3) The transition from the pleasure principle to the reality principle with all its ensuing ramifications for the psyche, schematically confined here to a single sentence, is actually achieved neither all at once nor along a uniform front. While the ego drives are undergoing

this development, the sexual drives diverge in a highly significant way. The sexual drives initially behave auto-erotically, finding their satisfaction in the subject's own body and therefore never experiencing the state of frustration that necessitated the introduction of the reality principle. Later, when they do begin the process of finding an object, this is promptly interrupted by the long latency period that delays sexual development until puberty. As a result of these two factors – auto-eroticism and latency – the sexual drive is arrested in its psychic development and continues to be ruled for much longer by the pleasure principle, in many people never managing to free itself from this at all.

As a result of these conditions, a closer relationship is established, on the one hand, between the sexual drive and fantasizing and, on the other, between the ego drives and the activities of consciousness. This relationship strikes us, in healthy and neurotic people alike, as a very intimate one, even if the above considerations of developmental psychology show it to be *secondary*. The continuing effects of auto-eroticism make it possible for the easier, instantaneous satisfaction of fantasizing about the sexual object to be retained for so long in place of real satisfaction, which involves making efforts and tolerating delays. Repression remains all-powerful in the realm of fantasy; it is able to inhibit ideas *in statu nascendi* – before they reach consciousness – if their being invested with energy could cause a release of unpleasure. This is the weak spot in our psychic organization that can be used to bring already rational thought processes back under the sway of the pleasure principle. Thus an essential element in the psyche's predisposition to neurosis results from the delay in educating the sexual drive to take account of reality, and from the conditions that make this delay possible.

4) Just as the pleasure-ego can do nothing but *wish*, pursue pleasure and avoid unpleasure, so the reality-ego has no other task than to strive for what is *useful* and to protect itself from what is harmful.[6] By taking over from the pleasure principle, the reality principle is really just safeguarding it, not deposing it. A momentary pleasure with uncertain consequences is given up, but only in order to obtain, by the new approach, a more secure pleasure later on.

Still, the endopsychic impact of this transition has been so powerful that it is reflected in a specific religious myth. The doctrine that the – voluntary or enforced – renunciation of earthly pleasures will be rewarded in the afterlife is simply the mythopoeic projection of this psychic transformation. Following this principle to its logical conclusion, *religions* have been able to bring about the absolute renunciation of pleasure in this life in return for the promise of recompense in a future existence; by so doing they have not conquered the pleasure principle. *Science* comes closest to achieving this conquest, but scientific work, too, provides intellectual pleasure and promises practical gain eventually.

5) *Education* can without question be described as an impetus to overcoming the pleasure principle and replacing it with the reality principle; thus it assists the process of development undergone by the ego. For this purpose, it uses the educators' love as a form of reward, and therefore goes awry when a spoilt child believes it possesses this love anyway and cannot lose it under any circumstances.

6) *Art* brings about a reconciliation of the two principles in a unique way. The artist is originally someone who, unable to come to terms with the renunciation of drive satisfaction initially demanded by reality, turns away from it and gives free rein to erotic and ambitious wishes in his fantasy life. Thanks to special gifts, however, he finds his way back to reality from this fantasy world by shaping his fantasies into new kinds of reality, which are appreciated by people as valid representations of the real world. Thus in a certain way he actually becomes the hero, king, creator, favourite he wanted to be, without having to make the enormous detour of actually changing the outside world. But he can achieve this only because other people feel the same dissatisfaction he does at the renunciations imposed by reality, and this dissatisfaction, a result of the transition from pleasure principle to reality principle, is itself an aspect of reality.[7]

7) As the ego undergoes the transformation from *pleasure-ego* into *reality-ego*, the sexual drives undergo the changes that lead from initial auto-eroticism, through various intermediate phases, to

object-love in the service of the reproductive function. If it is true that every stage along each of these two courses of development can become the site of a predisposition towards subsequent neurotic illness, it seems likely that the form this illness takes (the *choice of neurosis*) will depend on which phase of ego or libido development the predisposing arrest occurred in. The – as yet uninvestigated – chronological characteristics of these two developments, the possible variations in their respective rates of progress, thus take on a whole new significance.

8) The strangest characteristic of unconscious (repressed) processes, to which the investigator can become accustomed only by dint of great self-discipline, results from their total disregard for reality-testing; thought-reality is equated with external reality, the wish with its fulfilment, just as occurs spontaneously under the rule of the old pleasure principle. For this reason it is extremely difficult to distinguish between unconscious fantasies and memories that have become unconscious. But we should never be tempted to apply the criteria of reality to repressed psychic formations by, say, underestimating the role played by fantasies in the creation of symptoms just because they are not real, or by attributing a neurotic feeling of guilt to some other source because no actual crime can be ascertained. We have to use the currency that prevails in the country we are exploring – in our case, the *neurotic currency*. Suppose, for example, we try to decipher the following dream. A man, who had looked after his father during his long and agonizing fatal illness, reports having repeatedly dreamt in the months following his death: *his father was alive again and was talking with him as usual. But at the same time he felt extremely distressed that his father was indeed dead and was just unaware of the fact.* The only way to make this absurd-sounding dream comprehensible is to add, after 'that his father was indeed dead', the words 'as he had wished' or 'as a result of his wish', and, at the end, the words 'that he had wished for it'. The dream-thought, then, is as follows: It distresses him to remember how he was driven to wishing for his father's death (as a release) while he was still alive, and how awful it would be if his father had sensed this. So we are dealing with the familiar case of self-reproach

after the loss of a loved one, the reproach in this instance stemming from the significance of the death-wish against the father in infancy.

The shortcomings of this little essay – more introduction than exposition – are perhaps only slightly excused if I insist they were inevitable. In the few sentences on the psychic consequences of adapting to the reality principle, I had to touch on ideas that I would have preferred to hold back for now, and which will certainly require a great deal of effort to substantiate. Still, I hope well-disposed readers will recognize where in this work, too, I have had to bow to the reality principle.

(1911)

Notes

1. [P.] Janet [*Les névroses*, Paris] (1909).

2. Otto Rank has recently pointed out a remarkably clear intimation of this causality in Schopenhauer's *Die Welt als Wille und Vorstellung*. (See Rank ['Schopenhauer über den Wahnsinn'. *Zentbl. Psychoanal.* 1], 1910.)

3. The state of sleep replicates psychic life as it was before the recognition of reality, a prerequisite of sleep being the deliberate shutting out of reality (the sleep-wish).

4. I shall try to flesh out this schematic account with a few further remarks: It will rightly be objected that any organization devoted entirely to the pleasure principle, neglecting the reality of the outside world, could not survive for even the shortest time and so could not have arisen in the first place. Our recourse to a fiction like this can, however, be justified if we point out that the suckling infant very nearly embodies just such a psychic system, if we just include the maternal care. It probably hallucinates the fulfilment of its inner needs, then betrays its displeasure at the increasing stimulus and continued absence of satisfaction through the motor discharge of crying and flailing about, upon which it actually receives the satisfaction it had hallucinated. Later as a child it learns to use these discharge outlets as a deliberate means of expression. Since nursing is the prototype of all subsequent child-care, the rule of the pleasure principle can really come to an end only with a complete psychic detachment from the parents. – A nice example of a psychic system cut off from the stimuli of the outside world,

able to satisfy even its nutritional requirements autistically (to use Bleuler's term), is offered by the bird embryo with its food supply enclosed within the eggshell, maternal care being restricted to the provision of warmth. – I shall regard it as less a correction than an elaboration of the above scheme if it is required to include devices that enable the system living by the pleasure principle to withdraw from the stimuli of the real world. These devices simply correspond to 'repression', which treats inner unpleasurable stimuli as if they were external, projecting them into the outside world.

5. Just as a nation whose wealth is based on exploiting its natural resources sets aside a specific area, like Yellowstone Park, to be preserved in its wild state and spared from the changes brought about by civilization.

6. The superiority of the reality-ego over the pleasure-ego is aptly expressed in Bernard Shaw's words: 'To be able to choose the line of greatest advantage instead of yielding in the direction of least resistance.' (*Man and Superman: A Comedy and a Philosophy*.)

7. Cf. similar in O. Rank [*Der Künstler, Ansätze zu einer Sexualpsychologie*, Leipzig and Vienna] (1907).

Drives and Their Fates

We have often heard the demand that a science be built on clear and precisely defined basic concepts. In reality, no science, not even the most exact, starts out with such definitions. The true beginnings of scientific activity consist, rather, in the description of phenomena, which are then grouped, classified, and brought into relation with each other. Even when simply describing the material, we cannot avoid applying to it certain abstract ideas, acquired from somewhere or other but certainly not just from the new observations alone. When this material is further elaborated, such ideas – later the basic concepts of the science – are even more indispensable. They must initially have a certain degree of indeterminacy about them; there can be no question of clearly demarcating their content. While they exist in this state, we reach a consensus about their meaning by repeated reference to the empirical material from which they appear to derive but which, in reality, is being subordinated to them. Strictly speaking, then, they are in the nature of conventions – although everything actually depends on their being not chosen arbitrarily, but determined by meaningful connections with the empirical material, connections that, ostensibly, we surmise before we can properly identify and substantiate them. Only after a more thorough investigation of the relevant empirical field can we formulate its basic scientific concepts more precisely, progressively revising them to widen their applicability while keeping them completely free of contradictions. Then the time may also have come to try and pin them down in definitions. But the advance of knowledge will brook no rigidity here. As the example of physics strikingly demonstrates, even those 'basic concepts' firmly established in the form of definitions are constantly being substantially revised.

One such conventional, and at present still rather obscure, basic concept, which is none the less indispensable to us in psychology, is that of the *drive*. Let us try to flesh it out by considering it from a variety of angles.

First from the perspective of physiology. This has given us the concept of the *stimulus* and the model of the reflex, according to which a stimulus applied to living tissue (nerve substance) *from* the outside is discharged by action directed *towards* the outside. This action is appropriate in so far as it withdraws the stimulated substance from the influence of the stimulus, moving it out of reach of the stimulant effect.

So what is the relationship between 'drive' and 'stimulus'? There is nothing to prevent us from subsuming the concept of the drive under that of the stimulus: a drive, then, is a stimulus to the psyche. Straight away, though, we are mindful not simply to equate drive with psychic stimulus. Clearly there are other stimuli to the psyche than just drive stimuli – ones that behave much more like physiological stimuli. For example, when a strong light hits the eye, this is not a drive stimulus, but it is when we sense dryness in the mucous membrane of the throat, or irritation in the mucous membrane of the stomach.[1]

We now have the means to distinguish drive stimuli from other (physiological) stimuli acting on the psyche. First, a drive stimulus emanates not from the outside world, but from inside the organism itself. For this reason it affects the psyche differently and different actions are needed to remove it. Furthermore, we remain true to the essence of the stimulus if we assume it has the effect of a single impact; it can thus also be dealt with by a single expedient action, epitomized by motor flight from a source of stimulation. Of course, these impacts may be repeated and their effects may accumulate, but this does not alter our conception of the process of a stimulus or the conditions necessary for its removal. The effect of a drive, on the other hand, is never that of a *momentary* impact, but always that of a *constant* force. And because it impinges not from outside, but from inside the body, flight is of no avail against it. It is better to call the drive stimulus a 'need'; what removes this need is *'satisfaction'*. This can be achieved only by making a sufficient (adequate) alteration to the internal source of stimulation.

Suppose we adopt the standpoint of an almost completely helpless organism, not yet orientated in the world, whose nerve substance is receiving stimuli. This organism is very soon in a position to make a first distinction and achieve an initial orientation. On the one hand, it will discern stimuli that it can evade by muscle action (flight), stimuli it will ascribe to an outside world; on the other hand, there will be stimuli against which such action has no effect, whose characteristic constant pressure persists regardless; these stimuli are signs of an inner world, evidence of drive needs. The perceptual substance of the organism will thus have found, in the effectiveness of its muscle activity, a foothold in distinguishing an 'outside' from an 'inside'.

Initially, then, we locate the essence of the drive in its main characteristics – its emanating from sources of stimulation inside the organism, its manifesting itself as a constant force – and from these we deduce another of its features, its imperviousness to flight actions. In the course of this discussion, however, we cannot help noticing something that prompts a further admission from us. To guide us in our elaboration of psychological phenomena, not only do we bring, in the form of basic concepts, certain conventions to our empirical material, we also make use of a variety of complex *assumptions*. We have already alluded to the most important of these, it just remains for us to draw explicit attention to it. This assumption is *biological* in nature and involves the concept of purpose (or, perhaps, expediency); it runs as follows: the nervous system is an apparatus dedicated to eliminating the stimuli that reach it, or to reducing them to the lowest possible level; or an apparatus that, if it were only feasible, would aim to remain free from stimulation altogether. So, without, for the moment, taking exception to the vagueness of this idea, let us ascribe to the nervous system the task, broadly speaking, of *mastering stimuli*. Now we can see how greatly the introduction of drives complicates the simple model of the physiological reflex. External stimuli set the organism a single task, evasion; this is accomplished by muscle movements, one of which eventually achieves the aim and, being the most expedient, goes on to become an hereditary disposition. Drive stimuli, emanating from inside the organism, cannot be dealt with by this mechanism. They therefore make much greater demands on the nervous system, causing it to undertake intricate, convoluted activities that alter the outside world sufficiently for it to provide satisfaction to the inner source of stimulation; above all, they force the nervous system to renounce its ideal intention of avoiding stimuli because they supply a constant, inescapable flow of stimulation. Thus we may well conclude that it is not external stimuli, but the drives that are the real motive force behind the advances that have brought the nervous system, with its infinite capabilities, to its present height of development. Of course, there is nothing to prevent us from assuming that drives themselves are, at least in part, the precipitates of external stimuli, which over the course of phylogenesis have caused living tissue to modify.

If we now determine that the activity of even the most highly developed psychic apparatus is governed by the *pleasure principle*, i.e., regulated automatically by sensations on the pleasure–unpleasure scale, we can hardly avoid the further assumption that these sensations replicate the manner in which stimuli are dealt with – in the sense, no doubt, that an unpleasurable sensation involves an increase, a pleasurable sensation a decrease in stimulation. But we will be careful to preserve the extremely vague nature of this assumption until we can somehow manage to surmise the kinds of connection that exist between, on the one hand, pleasure and unpleasure and, on the other, fluctuations in the quantities of stimulation at work in the psyche. Such connections may well be very diverse and far from simple.

If we now turn to considering psychic life from the biological perspective, the 'drive' emerges as a concept on the borderline between the mental and the physical – the psychic representative of stimuli flowing into the psyche from inside the body, or the degree of workload imposed on the psyche as a result of its relation to the body.

❋

We can now discuss certain terms used in connection with the concept of the drive, such as its pressure, aim, object and source.

By the *pressure* of a drive we mean its motor element, the amount of force or the degree of workload it represents. Pressure is a general characteristic of the drives, indeed their very essence. Every drive involves activity; if we speak loosely of passive drives, this can mean only drives with a passive aim.

The *aim* of a drive is always satisfaction, which can be achieved only by removing the state of stimulation at the source of the drive. But even though this ultimate aim is invariable in every drive, a variety of means may lead to this same end, so that many different more or less intermediate aims may arise from a single drive, aims that can be combined and interchanged with one another. Experience also permits us to speak of '*aim-inhibited*' drives, where processes are allowed to advance some way towards drive satisfaction but are then inhibited or diverted. We can assume that these processes, too, involve partial satisfaction.

The *object* of a drive is that upon which or through which the drive is able to achieve its aim. It is the most variable aspect of a drive, not originally connected with it, but merely appropriated by it on grounds of its suitability to provide satisfaction. It is not necessarily something external, it can just as well be a part of the subject's own body. Over the course of a drive's unfolding fate, it may be changed as often as required, and this capacity for displacement has crucial roles to play. The same object may serve to satisfy a variety of drives simultaneously, a case of *overlapping* drives, as Alfred Adler (1908) puts it. A particularly intimate attachment of a drive to an object is classed as a *fixation* of that drive. This often occurs in very early phases of the drive's development, putting an end to the drive's mutability by vigorously resisting detachment from the object.

By the *source* of a drive we mean that physical process, in an organ or part of the body, whose stimulus is represented in the psyche by the drive. It is not known if this process is always chemical in nature or if it may also correspond with the release of other – for example, mechanical – forces. The study of drive sources goes beyond the scope of psychology; although a drive is wholly determined by its origin in a physical source, in psychic life it manifests itself only through its aims. More precise knowledge about drive sources is not strictly necessary for the purposes of psychological investigation. Sometimes we can confidently deduce the source of a drive from its aims.

Are we to assume that the various drives emanating from the body and acting on the psyche are also distinguished by various *qualities*, and thus behave in qualitatively different ways in psychic life? There does not appear to be any justification for this; rather the simpler assumption suffices – that the drives are all qualitatively alike and that it is the quantities of excitation they carry, perhaps also certain functions of this quantity, that alone are responsible for their effect. The differences in the psychic effects of individual drives can be traced back to their differing sources. It is, however, only in a later connection that we can explain the real significance of this question of drive qualities.

What drives, and how many, may we suppose exist? Clearly there is great scope here for arbitrariness. We cannot object to anyone resorting to the concept of a play drive, or a destruction drive, or a social drive, where the subject-matter calls for it and the limitations of psychological analysis permit. But we should not neglect to ask if such highly specialized drive motives cannot be further reduced to their sources, leaving only the irreducible primal drives to claim our interest.

I have proposed that we distinguish two groups of such primal drives, the *ego* or *self-preservation drives* and the *sexual drives*. This hypothesis does not, however, carry the weight of a necessary premise, unlike, for example, our assumption about the biological purpose of the psychic apparatus (see above); it is merely a kind of scaffolding, to be retained only as long as it proves useful and which can be replaced without greatly affecting the results of our work of description and classification. This hypothesis is a result of the historical evolution of psychoanalysis, which was initially applied to the psychoneuroses, specifically the group termed 'transference neuroses' (hysteria and compulsion neurosis). Here we came to the conclusion that at the root of every such illness lay a conflict between the demands of sexuality and those of the ego. It is always possible that an in-depth study of the other neurotic conditions (especially the narcissistic psychoneuroses, the schizophrenic disorders) could force us to revise this formula and consequently our classification of the primal drives. For now, though, we do not know this new formula, nor have we met with any argument that undermines our opposition of ego and sexual drives.

It is highly doubtful that conclusive pointers for differentiating and classifying the drives can ever be obtained just from elaborating the psychological material. It seems, rather, that for the purposes of this elaboration we need to apply definite assumptions about the nature of the drives to the material, and it would be preferable if we could take these assumptions from another field, transferring them to psychology. What biology has to contribute here certainly does not run counter to our distinction between ego drives and sexual drives. Biology informs us that sexuality is distinct from the other functions of the individual because its purposes – the creation of new individuals, and thus the preservation of the species – transcend the individual. It also shows us that two equally valid ways of conceiving of the relationship between ego and sexuality exist side by side, one in which the individual is paramount, with sexuality regarded as one of its activities and sexual satisfaction as one of its needs, and another according to which the individual is a temporary and transient adjunct to the quasi-immortal germ plasm entrusted to it in the process of reproduction. The assumption that the sexual function is distinguished from other bodily processes by a special chemistry is also, as I understand it, a premise of the Ehrlich school of biology.

As any study of the drives from the perspective of consciousness presents almost insurmountable difficulties, psychoanalytical research into psychic disorders remains the primary source of our knowledge. Due to the way it has evolved, though, psychoanalysis has so far been able to provide reasonably satisfactory information about only the sexual drives, having been able to observe only this particular group in isolation, as it were, in the psychoneuroses. No doubt the extension of psychoanalysis to the other neurotic conditions will provide us with the basis for a knowledge of the ego drives, although it seems presumptuous to expect similarly favourable conditions for observation in this new field of research.

To characterize the sexual drives in general, we can say the following: they are many in number, they emanate from a great variety of organic sources, and initially they act independently of each other, achieving a more or less complete synthesis only at a late stage. The aim each one strives to attain is *organ pleasure*; only on completing synthesis do they enter the service of the *reproductive function*, at which point they become generally recognizable as sexual drives. Initially, they are dependent on self-preservation drives and become detached from these only gradually; when finding an object, they also follow the paths laid down by the ego drives. A proportion of them remain attached to the ego drives throughout life, providing these with *libidinal* components, which are easily overlooked during normal functioning and manifest themselves only in illness. They have an extraordinary capacity to stand in vicariously for one another and to change their objects with ease. Due to these latter qualities, they are capable of feats far removed from their original functions. (*Sublimation.*)

Our investigation into the various fates experienced by drives over the course of their development and subsequent existence will have to be restricted to the better-known sexual drives. From our observations we know of the following such fates:

– Reversal into the opposite.
– Turning back on the self.
– Repression.
– Sublimation.

As I do not intend to deal with sublimation here, and repression requires a chapter of its own, it just remains for us to describe and discuss the first two items. In view of the forces at work to prevent drives from pursuing their direct course, we can also regard these fates as forms of *defence* against the drives.

On closer inspection, *reversal into the opposite* can be broken down into two different processes, *turning activity into passivity* and *reversal of content*. The two processes, being different in nature, must also be dealt with separately.

Examples of the first process are provided by the pairs of opposites sadism–masochism and voyeurism–exhibitionism. The reversal involves only the *aims* of the drive; the active aim (to hurt, to look at) is replaced by the passive aim (to be hurt, to be looked at). Reversal of content is found only in the case of the transformation of love into hate.

Turning back on the self is evident when we consider that masochism is really a form of sadism turned against the subject's own ego, or that exhibitionism includes looking at one's own body. Analytical observation leaves us in no doubt that the masochist does indeed share pleasure in the violence against himself, and that the exhibitionist shares pleasure in the act of exposure. The essence of the process, then, is the change of *object*, the aim remaining unchanged.

It cannot have escaped our notice that turning back on the self and turning activity into passivity correspond or coincide in these examples. To clarify these relations a more thorough investigation is necessary.

For the pair of opposites sadism–masochism we can represent the process as follows:

a) Sadism consists in exercising violence towards or power over another person, the object.

b) This object is relinquished and replaced by the subject's own person. With this turning back on the self, the active aim of the drive is transformed into a passive one.

c) Another person is once again sought as an object who, because the drive aim has been transformed, must now adopt the role of the subject.

Case *c* is that commonly known as masochism. Here, too, the satisfaction occurs along the path of the original sadism, the passive ego fantasizing itself back into its previous role, now ceded to the other subject. It is highly unlikely that a more direct form of masochistic satisfaction exists. A primary masochism – one that does

21

not stem from sadism in the way described above – does not appear to occur.[2] That the postulation of stage *b* is not superfluous is clear from the behaviour of the sadistic drive in compulsion neurosis. Here we find turning back on the self but without passivity towards another person. The transformation proceeds only as far as stage *b*. The desire for cruelty turns into self-torment and self-punishment, not masochism. The active verb becomes not a passive, but a reflexive.

Our view of sadism is further complicated by the fact that, alongside (or perhaps, rather, within) its general aim, this drive seems to strive for a quite special aim. As well as to humiliate and dominate, it seeks to inflict pain. Psychoanalysis, however, seems to show that inflicting pain plays no part in the drive's original aims. The sadistic child pays no heed to whether it inflicts pain or not and never intends to do so. Once the transformation into masochism has taken place, however, pain is very well suited to becoming a passive masochistic aim, for we have every reason to believe that sensations of pain can – like other sensations of unpleasure – shade over into sexual arousal and produce a pleasurable state, for the sake of which even the unpleasure of pain can be willingly undergone. Once feeling pain has become a masochistic aim, the sadistic aim of inflicting pain can also arise retroactively, for this pain, while being caused to another person, is enjoyed masochistically in identification with the suffering object. In both cases, of course, it is not the pain itself that is enjoyed, but the accompanying sexual arousal, which is especially convenient for the sadist. This would make the enjoyment of pain a primary masochistic aim, but one which can become a drive aim only in someone who was originally sadistic.

For the sake of completeness, I should add that *compassion* cannot be described as the result of a transformation of the sadistic drive, but involves instead the notion of a *reaction formation* against the drive (for the difference, see later).

The study of another pair of opposites, the drives whose aims are looking and displaying oneself (voyeurism and exhibitionism, in the language of the perversions), yields somewhat different and simpler results. Here, too, we can postulate the same stages as in the previous case: *a)* looking as an *activity* directed towards another object; *b)* relinquishing the object, turning the voyeuristic drive towards a part of one's own body and, with this, reversal into passivity and the setting up of a new aim – to be looked at; *c)* the introduction of a new subject to whom one displays oneself in order to be looked at. Again we can hardly doubt that the active aim occurs before the passive one, that looking precedes being looked at. There is, however, a significant deviation from the paradigm of sadism in that we can detect in the voyeuristic drive an even earlier stage than that designated *a*. In its initial activity the voyeuristic drive is auto-erotic – it does have an object, but one found on the subject's own body. Only later does it come (by way of comparison) to exchange this object for an analogous one on the body of another (stage *a*). This preliminary stage is interesting because the situations of each of the resulting pair of opposites arise from it, depending on which element is transformed. A diagram for the voyeuristic drive might look as follows:

a) Looking at one's sexual organ = Sexual organ being looked at by oneself

| |

β) Looking at an external object   *γ)* Being the object looked at by another
   (active voyeurism)   (exhibitionism).

A preliminary stage of this kind is not present in sadism, which from the outset is directed towards an external object, although it would not exactly be absurd to construct such a stage from the child's efforts to gain mastery over its own limbs.[3]

It is true of both kinds of drive under consideration here that transformations by reversal of activity into passivity and turning back on the self never actually involve the whole amount of the drive impulse. To some extent, the older, active tendency continues to exist alongside the later, passive one, even when the transformation has been very extensive. The only accurate statement we could make about the voyeuristic drive is that all its developmental stages – the preliminary auto-erotic stage as well as its final active and passive forms – coexist alongside each other, which becomes evident when we take as our basis not the actions prompted by the drive, but the mechanism of satisfaction. Perhaps we might permit ourselves to consider and depict these circumstances in yet another way. We can divide the life of each drive up into individual waves – temporally distinct and uniform within any given period – which behave in relation to each other somewhat like successive eruptions of lava. We might then imagine, say, the first, original eruption of the drive continuing in an unchanged form, undergoing no development of any kind. A subsequent wave may then, from the outset, undergo some change – reversal into passivity, say – and would then add itself, with this new characteristic, to the previous one, and so on. If we were then to survey the drive impulse from its beginning up to a given point, this succession of waves would offer us an image of the specific development of that drive.

The fact that, in this later period of development, a drive impulse can be observed alongside its (passive) opposite merits its own special term, for which Bleuler's *ambivalence* is ideal.

These considerations of the genesis of drives and the permanence of their intermediate stages provide us with some understanding of the way drives have developed. Experience shows that the degree of demonstrable ambivalence varies greatly between individuals, groups and races. A marked drive ambivalence in someone alive today may be regarded as an archaic inheritance, because we have reason to believe that untransformed, active drive impulses generally played a greater role in primeval times than today.

We have taken to calling the early phase of the ego's development, during which the sexual drives find satisfaction auto-erotically, *narcissism* (avoiding, at first, any discussion about the relationship between auto-eroticism and narcissism). This would mean the preliminary stage of the voyeuristic drive, in which the object of the desire to look is the subject's own body, would have to be classed under narcissism, as a narcissistic formation. The active voyeuristic drive would then evolve from this by leaving narcissism behind, whereas passive voyeurism would retain the narcissistic object. Similarly, the transformation of sadism into masochism would involve a reversion to the narcissistic object, in both cases the narcissistic subject being replaced, via identification, by another, external ego. Taking our construction of a preliminary narcissistic stage of sadism into account, we approach the more general conclusion that these two drive fates – turning back on the self and reversal of activity into passivity – are dependent on the narcissistic organization of the ego and bear the imprint of this phase. Perhaps they represent attempts at defence that at higher levels of ego development are conducted by other means.

Let us remind ourselves at this point that we have so far discussed only two pairs of drive opposites: sadism–masochism and voyeurism–exhibitionism. These are the best-known sexual drives that occur ambivalently. The other components of what is later to become the sexual function are not yet sufficiently accessible to analysis for us to be able to discuss them in a similar way. We can say of them in general that their activity is *auto-erotic*, i.e., their object is insignificant in comparison with the organ that is their source, and as a rule the two coincide. The object of the voyeuristic drive, although initially also a part of the subject's own body, is not however the eye itself, and the organ at the source of sadism – probably the system of muscles capable of action – points directly towards another object, even if this is part of the subject's own body. The organ at its source is so crucial to an auto-erotic drive that, according to an appealing hypothesis proposed by P. Federn (1913) and L. Jekels (1913), the form and function of the organ determine the activity or passivity of the drive aim.

The reversal of a drive's content into its opposite can be observed in just one case, the *transformation of love into hate*. These two are so commonly directed towards the same object simultaneously that this coexistence also provides us with the most significant example of emotional ambivalence.

The case of love and hate is particularly interesting in that it resists being assimilated into our account of the drives. We cannot doubt that the most intimate relationship exists between these two emotional opposites and sexuality, but we naturally reject the notion that love is some specific component drive of sexuality like any other. We would prefer to view love as the expression of the sexual urge as a whole, but this is also insufficient, and we are not sure how we are to understand the opposite of this urge.

Love has not just one, but three opposites. Apart from the opposition of loving–hating, there is another of loving–being loved and, in addition, loving and hating taken together stand in opposition to indifference. The second of these three oppositions, that of loving–being loved, corresponds exactly with the transformation of activity into passivity and can, like the voyeuristic drive, also be traced back to a primal situation. This is *loving oneself*, which for us is the characteristic feature of narcissism. Depending on whether the object or the subject is then exchanged for an external one, there results the active aim of loving or the passive aim of being loved, the latter remaining close to narcissism.

We can perhaps better understand the various opposites of love by reflecting that our psychic life as a whole is governed by *three polarities*, the oppositions of:

– *subject (ego)–object (outside world)*

– *pleasure–unpleasure*

– *active–passive*.

As we have already said, the opposition of ego–non-ego (outside), or subject–object, impresses itself on the individual organism at an early stage, when it learns that it can silence external stimuli by its muscle actions but is defenceless against drive stimuli. It is an opposition that, above all, governs intellectual activity, creating the basic condition of scientific investigation that no amount of effort can alter. The polarity of pleasure–unpleasure is based on a scale of sensations whose supremely significant role in deciding our actions (will) has already been stressed. The opposition of active–passive is not to be confused with that of ego-subject–outside-object. The ego behaves passively towards the outside world in so far as it receives stimuli from it, but actively when it reacts to these. It is forced into especial *activity* towards the outside world by its drives, so we could, in emphasizing what is essential, say the ego-subject is passive towards external stimuli, but active through its own drives. The opposition active–passive later converges with that of masculine–feminine, which has no psychological significance prior to this. The fusion of activity with masculinity and passivity with femininity presents itself to us as nothing less than a biological fact; it is, however, by no means as invariably comprehensive or exclusive as we tend to assume.

The three psychic polarities are interconnected in crucial ways. There is one primal psychic situation in which two of them coincide. Originally, at the very beginning of psychic life, the ego finds itself invested with drives that it is able, in part, to satisfy by itself. We call this state narcissism and this means of satisfaction auto-erotic.[4] The outside world at this time is not invested with interest (in the general sense) and remains a matter of indifference as far as satisfaction is concerned. At this time, then, the ego-subject coincides with what is pleasurable, the outside world with what is indifferent (or possibly, as a source of stimulation, with what is unpleasurable). If we initially define love as the ego's relation to its sources of pleasure, the situation in which the ego loves only itself, and is indifferent to the world, accounts for the first opposition in which love occurs.

In so far as it is auto-erotic, the ego does not need the outside world, but, as a result of experiences undergone by the self-preservation drives, it does acquire objects from it, and of course it cannot help perceiving inner drive stimuli as temporarily unpleasurable. So under the rule of the pleasure principle another development now takes place. The ego takes the objects it encounters, in so far as they are sources of pleasure, into itself, it introjects them (to use Ferenczi's term), while, on the other hand, expelling whatever within itself causes unpleasure. (See later, the mechanism of projection.)

The original reality-ego, which distinguished an inside from an outside by means of a sound objective criterion, thus turns into a purified *pleasure-ego*, which puts the factor of pleasure above all else. The outside world is divided up into a pleasurable part, which it incorporates into itself, and the rest, which is alien to it. It also separates off a part of its own self, which it projects into the outside world and perceives as hostile. After this rearrangement, the congruence is restored between the two polarities:

– ego-subject and pleasure

– outside world and unpleasure (previously indifference).

When objects appear during the stage of primary narcissism, the second opposite of love develops as well, namely hate.

As we have heard, the ego is first introduced to objects from the outside world by the self-preservation drives, and we have to accept that hate originally denoted the ego's relation to the alien outside world and its stimuli. After having first appeared as their forerunner, indifference must now be classed as a special case of hate or aversion. In the very beginning, the outside world, objects, and what is hated are identical. If an object subsequently proves to be a source of pleasure, it is loved, but it is also incorporated into the ego, so, for the purified pleasure-ego, the object and what is alien and hated are once again one and the same.

Now, however, we note that, just as the opposition of love–indifference mirrors the polarity of ego–outside world, so the second opposition of love–hate reflects the related polarity of pleasure–unpleasure. When the purely narcissistic stage has been superseded by the object stage, pleasure and unpleasure denote the ego's relations to objects. If an object is a source of pleasurable sensations, there arises a motor impulse to bring it closer to and incorporate it into the ego; we then speak of the 'attraction' of the pleasure-giving object and say we 'love' the object. Conversely, if the object is a source of unpleasurable sensations, there is an impulse to increase the distance between it and the ego, repeating the original attempt at flight from the stimuli of the outside world. We feel 'repulsion' at such an object and hate it; this hate can then escalate into an aggressive inclination towards the object, an intent to destroy it.

We could, at a stretch, say that a drive 'loves' the object that it strives towards in search of satisfaction. But to say a drive 'hates' an object sounds strange to us, so we see the terms love and hate do not apply to the relations between drives and their objects and should be reserved for the relation of the ego as a whole to its objects. However, considerations of linguistic usage, which are no doubt significant, reveal a further limitation to the meaning of love and hate. We do not say that we love the objects that serve self-preservation, rather we emphasize the fact that we need them, perhaps expanding on this by using words that indicate a highly subdued form of love, such as liking, being fond of, finding pleasant.

The word 'love', then, shifts ever more into the sphere of the ego's pure relation of pleasure to the object, finally affixing itself to sexual objects in the narrower sense, as well as to those objects satisfying the needs of sublimated sexual drives. The distinction between ego and sexual drives that we have imposed on our psychology thus proves to be in keeping with the spirit of our language. If we do not normally say a particular sexual drive loves its object, and if the most appropriate use of the word 'love' is, rather, to describe the ego's relation to its sexual object, this tells us that the word is applicable here only after the synthesis of all the component sexual drives under the primacy of the genitals in the service of the reproductive function.

It is worth noting that no such intimate connection with sexual pleasure and the sexual function is evident in our use of the word 'hate'; the relation of unpleasure seems, rather, to be the sole decisive factor. The ego hates, is repelled by, pursues with destructive intent any object that becomes a source of unpleasurable sensations, regardless of whether it is frustrating sexual satisfaction or the satisfaction of self-preservation needs. Indeed, we can say that the true prototypes of the hate relation stem not from sexual life, but from the ego's struggle to preserve and assert itself.

Love and hate, then, which present themselves to us as complete opposites, stand in no such simple relation to each other after all. They have not originated from the splitting up of some primal common entity, but have different sources and have undergone separate developments before being constituted as opposites under the influence of pleasure–unpleasure relations. We are now left with the task of summarizing what we know about the genesis of love and hate.

Love stems from the ego's capacity to satisfy some of its drive impulses auto-erotically, by the attainment of organ pleasure. It is originally narcissistic, then it spreads to those objects incorporated into the extended ego, expressing the ego's motor impulse towards these objects as sources of pleasure. It becomes intimately related to the activity of the later sexual drives and, when their synthesis is complete, corresponds to the sexual urge as a whole. The preliminary stages of love manifest themselves as provisional sexual aims while the sexual drives undergo their complex development. We know the first of these aims to be *incorporating* or *devouring*, a form of love compatible with putting an end to the object's existence as a separate entity, one which can therefore be described as ambivalent. At the higher stage of pregenital sadistic-anal organization, desire for the object manifests itself in the form of an urge to overpower it, regardless of whether this causes injury or destruction to the object. In its treatment of the object, then, this form and preliminary stage of love is scarcely distinguishable from hate. Only after the establishment of the genital organization does love become the opposite of hate.

As an object relation, hate is older than love, its source being the narcissistic ego's primal rejection of the stimuli of the outside world. As an expression of the reaction of unpleasure provoked by objects, it remains forever closely related to the self-preservation drives, so that ego drives and sexual drives readily form an opposition replicating that between hate and love. When the ego drives dominate the sexual function, as at the stage of sadistic-anal organization, they also lend the characteristics of hate to the drive aims.

The history of love's origins and relations explains why it so often occurs in 'ambivalent' form, i.e., accompanied by impulses of hate towards the same object. The admixture of hate in love derives in part from the preliminary stages of love that have not been fully surmounted, the rest being based on reactions of rejection by the ego drives, which, in view of the frequent conflicts between self-interest and love interests, can adduce real and present motives. In both cases, then, the admixture of hate can be traced back to a source in the self-preservation drives. When a love relation towards a particular object is broken off, hate not infrequently takes its place, giving us the impression that love has turned into hate. We go one better than this description with our view that the presently motivated hate is here being bolstered by the regression of love to the preliminary sadistic stage, providing the hate with an erotic character and ensuring the continuation of a love relation.

The third opposition involving love, the transformation of loving into being loved, corresponds to the influence of the polarity of activity and passivity and can be viewed in the same way as the cases of voyeurism and sadism.

We may conclude by pointing out that the drive fates consist essentially in *drive impulses being subjected to the influence of the three great polarities governing psychic life*. Of these three polarities, that of activity–passivity could be described as the *biological* polarity, that of ego–outside world as the *real* polarity, and finally that of pleasure–unpleasure as the *economic* polarity.

The drive fate of *repression* will be the subject of the following study.

(1915)

Notes

1. Assuming these internal processes are indeed the organic basis of the needs of thirst and hunger respectively.
2. In connection with problems regarding the life of the drives, I have in later works (see 'The Economic Problem of Masochism', 1924) expressed the opposite view.
3. See previous note.
4. Certain of the sexual drives are, as we know, capable of this auto-erotic satisfaction and are therefore suitable vehicles of the development governed by the pleasure principle to be described presently. Of course, those sexual drives requiring an object from the outset and those needs based on ego drives, which can never be satisfied auto-erotically, disrupt the primal narcissistic state, paving the way for progress. Indeed, this state could not even undergo that development at all were it not for the fact that each individual organism passes through a period of *helplessness* and *nurture*, during which its urgent needs are satisfied by an outside agency and are thus withdrawn from the process of development.

Repression

Repression

One fate that a drive impulse can experience is to run up against resistances seeking to put it out of action. Under certain conditions, which we shall now investigate more closely, it then enters the state of *repression*. If it were a case of the effect of an external stimulus, the appropriate measure would obviously be flight. In the case of a drive, flight is of no avail, since the ego cannot escape from itself. At a later stage, judicious rejection (*disapproval*) is found to be a good measure against drive impulses. A preliminary stage of this disapproval, something between flight and disapproval, is repression – a concept that could not have been formulated in the days before psychoanalytical studies.

It is not easy to deduce theoretically why repression is possible. Why should a drive impulse be subject to such a fate? Evidently a precondition here is that achieving the drive aim would bring unpleasure instead of pleasure. But it is not easy to conceive of such a situation. Such drives do not exist – the satisfaction of a drive is always pleasurable. We would need to assume the existence of special circumstances, some process or other that transforms the pleasure of satisfaction into unpleasure.

To delineate repression more clearly, we can look at certain other situations involving drives. It can happen that an external stimulus becomes internalized – for example, by attacking and destroying an organ – resulting in a new source of constant excitation and increased tension. Thus it becomes something very similar to a drive. We know this situation is experienced as *pain*. The aim of this pseudo-drive, though, is simply to put an end to the change in the organ and the unpleasure accompanying it. No other, more direct pleasure can be gained from stopping the pain. Pain is also imperative; it can other-wise be allayed only by an analgesic or by mental distraction.

Pain is too impenetrable a case to serve our present purposes. Let us take the case of a drive stimulus, such as hunger, that remains unsatisfied. It then becomes imperative – it can be alleviated only by the act of satisfaction and it maintains the constant tension characteristic of a need. There appears to be absolutely no scope here for anything like repression.

Repression, then, certainly does not ensue from tension reaching intolerable levels due to the non-satisfaction of a drive impulse. The defensive measures available to the organism in this situation must be dealt with in another context.

Let us restrict ourselves to clinical experience as met with in psychoanalytical practice. Here we learn that drives under repression are indeed capable of satisfaction, and that this would always, in itself, be pleasurable, but it would be irreconcilable with other demands and intentions; so it would produce pleasure in one place, unpleasure in another. Thus it becomes a precondition of repression that the motive of avoiding unpleasure overrides the pleasure of satisfaction. Our experience of transference neuroses in psychoanalysis leads us further to conclude that repression is not one of the original defence mechanisms, that it cannot occur until a sharp division has been established between conscious and uncon-scious psychic activity, and that *its essence consists simply in the act of turning – and keeping – something away from the conscious*. We may round this conception of repression out by assuming that, prior to this stage of psychic organization, the task of defence against drive impulses was dealt with by the other drive fates, such as reversal into the opposite and turning back on the self.

We also realize now that repression and the unconscious are so closely correlated that we must defer any in-depth study into the nature of repression until we know more about the structure of the series of agencies in the psyche and the distinction between unconscious and conscious. Until then, all we can do is gather together, purely descriptively, some of the characteristics of repression known to us from clinical practice, even though we run the risk of repeating word for word much that has been said elsewhere.

So, we have reason to assume the existence of a *primal repression*, an initial phase of repression that consists in the psychic (ideational) representative of the drive being denied access to the conscious. This establishes a *fixation*; from then on, that particular drive representative continues to exist unchanged and the drive remains attached to it. This is due to the special properties of unconscious processes, to be discussed later.

The second stage of repression, *actual repression*, affects psychic derivatives of the repressed representative, or trains of thought that, though originating elsewhere, have become associated with it. Because of this relationship, these ideas experience the same fate as the primally repressed material. Actual repression, then, is a kind of follow-up repression. Incidentally, it would be wrong to put all the emphasis on the repulsion exerted from the conscious on the material to be repressed. Equally significant is the attraction that the primally repressed material exerts on everything with which it can associate itself. The repressive tendency probably could not achieve its aim if these two forces were not working hand in hand and there were no previously repressed material ready to take up what is repelled from the conscious.

Influenced by our study of the psychoneuroses, where we see its profound effects, we tend to overestimate the psychological impact of repression and forget too easily that it does not prevent the drive representative from continuing to exist in the unconscious, from undergoing further organization, from forming derivatives, or from making new connections. Repression actually affects the drive representative only in its relationship to one psychic system – the conscious.

Psychoanalysis can reveal more that helps us understand the effects of repression in the psychoneuroses. We know, for example, that if a drive representative is removed by repression from the influence of the conscious, it develops more rampantly and exuberantly. It proliferates in the dark, so to speak, and finds extreme forms of expression, which, when translated and presented to the neurotic, not only are bound to appear alien to him, but also frighten him by making the drive seem so extraordinary and dangerous in its intensity. This deceptive intensity is a result of the drive's uninhibited development in fantasy and the build-up caused by lack of satisfaction. The fact that repression has this latter effect points us in the direction of its true significance.

To return to the opposite perspective, though, we should make it clear that repression does not even keep all derivatives of primally repressed material away from the conscious. If they are far enough removed from the repressed representative, whether by distortion or by the number of mediating interpolations, then they can have free access to the conscious. It is as if the resistance against them from the conscious were a function of their remoteness from the originally repressed material. When applying the technique of psychoanalysis, we continually ask the patient to produce derivatives of the repressed that are sufficiently remote or distorted to get past the censorship of the conscious. Precisely these are the associations that we demand he produce while abandoning all conscious intentions and all criticism, and from which we reproduce a conscious translation of the repressed representative. We observe here that the patient can go on spinning out a thread of associations like this until at some point he comes across a thought formation so heavily intertwined with connections to the repressed that he has to repeat his attempted repression. Neurotic symptoms must also have fulfilled the same condition because they, too, are derivatives of the repressed, which latter has, by way of these formations, finally wrested the access to consciousness previously denied it.

We cannot generalize about how distorted or remote from the repressed something must become for resistance from the conscious to be lifted. A subtle weighing-up takes place, whose action is hidden from us but whose effects allow us to guess that it is a question of intervention occurring when the unconscious investment reaches a certain intensity beyond which it would force its way through to satisfaction. Repression thus operates in a *highly individual* way; each individual derivative of the repressed can have its own particular fate; a little more distortion or a little less can reverse the whole outcome. It is in this connection that we can understand how our most cherished objects – our ideals – stem from the same perceptions and experiences as those we most abhor, and how originally the two differed from each other only by virtue of slight modifications. Indeed, as we discovered in the case of the origin of fetishes, the original drive representative can be split in two, one part undergoing repression while the other, precisely due to this intimate association, experiences the fate of idealization.

That which can be achieved by increases and decreases in distortion can also be achieved at the other end of the apparatus, so to speak, by modifications in the conditions of pleasure and unpleasure production. Special techniques have evolved, the purpose of which is to modulate the play of forces in the psyche so that material which normally generates unpleasure can yield pleasure; and whenever such a technique comes into operation, the repression of an otherwise rejected drive representative is lifted. So far, these techniques have been studied in detail only in the case of *jokes*. As a rule, the repression is lifted only temporarily; it is promptly re-established.

Observations of this kind can, however, make us aware of other characteristics of repression. Not only is it, as we have just shown, *individual*, it is also extremely *mobile*. We should not think of the process of repression as a single event with permanent results, as when, say, a living thing is killed and from then on remains dead; repression demands, rather, a constant expenditure of energy and would be undermined if this were relaxed, necessitating a renewed act of repression. We may imagine the repressed exerting continuous pressure in the direction of the conscious, and this must be held in equilibrium by an unrelenting counterpressure. Maintaining a repression, then, requires a constant expenditure of energy, whereas lifting it represents, in economic terms, a saving. Incidentally, the mobility of repression is also apparent in the psychic characteristics of the state of sleep, which alone makes the formation of dreams possible. When we wake up, the withdrawn investments of repressive energy are once again sent out.

We should not forget that, ultimately, we have said very little about a drive impulse simply by stating it to be repressed. Repression notwithstanding, it can exist in a wide variety of states – it can be inactive, i.e., invested with very little psychic energy, or it can be invested with energy to varying degrees and so capable of activity. True, its activation will not cause the repression to be lifted directly, but it will galvanize all those processes that, by circuitous routes, ultimately break through to consciousness. For unrepressed derivatives of the unconscious, the fate of a particular idea is often determined by the degree of its activation or investment. It is perfectly common for such a derivative to remain unrepressed as long as it represents only a small quantity of energy, even if the nature of its content would normally bring it into conflict with the ruling trend in the conscious. The quantitative factor proves decisive in this conflict; as soon as the fundamentally offensive idea reaches a certain level of intensity, the conflict becomes active, and precisely this activation elicits repression. Where repression is concerned, then, increased investment has the same effect as increased proximity to the unconscious, while decreases have the same effect as remoteness from it or distortion. We see that the repressive tendencies can, as a substitute for repressing something unpleasant, simply reduce its intensity.

In our discussion so far, we have dealt with the repression of the drive representative, which we have taken to mean an idea or group of ideas invested with a certain quantity of energy (libido, interest) from the drive. Clinical observation now forces us to dissect what we have so far conceived of as a whole, because it reveals to us that, besides the idea, something else representing the drive must be taken into consideration, and this other element can, when repressed, experience a fate quite distinct from that of the idea. We have taken to calling this other element of the psychic representative the *emotive charge*; it is the part of the drive that can become detached from the idea and find an expression commensurate with its quantity in processes that are experienced as emotions. From now on when describing a case of repression, we shall have to keep track of what becomes of each separate repressed element, the idea and the drive energy attached to it.

We should like to say something general about the fates of each of these, and, having taken our bearings a little, we can do just this. The general fate of the *idea* representing the drive can hardly be anything but to disappear from consciousness if it was previously conscious, or to be kept away from consciousness if it was about to become so. The distinction is not important; it amounts more or less to the difference between throwing an unpleasant guest out of my drawing-room or hallway, and, having recognized who it is, not letting him through the front door at all.[1] A brief survey of psychoanalytical experience tells us that the *quantitative* element of the drive representative can experience three kinds of fate: the drive is either completely suppressed so that no trace of it is visible, or it manifests itself as an emotion coloured by some or other quality, or it is transformed into anxiety. These two latter possibilities set us the task of considering the *transformation* of the psychic energies of *drives* into *emotions* – especially *anxiety* – as a new kind of drive fate.

We recall that the sole motive and purpose of repression is to avoid unpleasure. It follows that the fate of the emotive charge of the drive representative is far more important than that of the idea, and it is this that determines the success or otherwise of the process of repression. If a repression does not manage to prevent feelings of unpleasure or anxiety from arising, we may say it has failed, even if it has achieved its aim as far as the ideational element is concerned. Naturally, failed repressions will be of more interest to us than successful ones, which for the most part will elude our scrutiny.

We now want to gain some insight into the *mechanism* of the process of repression, and we especially want to know if there is just one mechanism of repression, or several, and whether perhaps each of the psychoneuroses has its own distinctive mechanism of repression. But this investigation runs into complications from the outset. The mechanism of a repression is accessible to us only by inference from its effects. If we restrict our observations to its effects on the ideational element of the representative, we find, as a rule, that repression creates a *substitute formation*. What, then, is the mechanism of these substitute formations – or are there several distinct mechanisms here, too? We also know that repression generates *symptoms*. Can we regard substitute formation and symptom formation as one and the same, and if, on the whole, we can, is the mechanism of symptom formation identical to that of repression? Tentatively, we can say the likelihood is that the two are very different, and that it is not repression itself that creates substitute formations and symptoms, but rather that these latter signify a *return of the repressed* and so owe their existence to very different processes. It would also seem advisable to examine the mechanisms of substitute and symptom formation before we tackle those of repression.

Clearly, speculation can be of no further use and must now give way to a careful analysis of the observable effects of repression in each of the individual neuroses. However, I must suggest that we also postpone this task until we have formed a reliable conception of the relationship between the conscious and the unconscious. To prevent this discussion from proving entirely unproductive, let me say straight away (1) that the mechanism of repression is not, in fact, the same as the mechanism of substitute formation, (2) that there are many, very diverse mechanisms of substitute formation, and (3) that the mechanisms of repression have at least one thing in common – the *withdrawal of the energy investment* (or, in the case of sexual drives, the *libido*).

Restricting myself to examples taken from the three best-known psychoneuroses, I would also like to show how the above concepts can be applied to the study of repression. From *anxiety hysteria*, I shall take a well-analysed example of an animal phobia. The drive impulse under repression here is a libidinal attitude towards the father, coupled with fear of him. After repression, this impulse disappears from consciousness – the father is no longer present here as a libidinal object. As a substitute in a parallel situation, there appears an animal more or less suitable as an object of anxiety. This substitute for the ideational element has been formed by means of *displacement* along a specifically determined association. The quantitative element has not disappeared, but has been transformed into anxiety. The result is that a need for love from the father is replaced by a fear of wolves. Of course, the categories used here are insufficient to provide an adequate explanation of even the simplest case of psychoneurosis. Various other aspects must always be taken into account.

In the case of animal phobia, the repression may be described as thoroughly unsuccessful. Its only achievement is to remove the idea and replace it with a substitute; the avoidance of unpleasure has failed completely. For this reason, the work of the neurosis does not end, but proceeds to a second phase in order to achieve its primary, more important aim. This leads to the formation of an attempted flight – the actual *phobia*, comprising a number of avoidances intended to preclude any release of anxiety. A more specialized investigation will provide us with an understanding of the mechanism by which the phobia achieves its aim.

The picture presented to us by true *conversion hysteria* requires a quite different assessment of the process of repression. The salient feature here is that the emotive charge can be made to disappear entirely. The patient then exhibits towards his symptoms what Charcot called '*la belle indifférence des hystériques*'. On other occasions, this suppression is not so completely successful – some distressing feelings attach to the symptoms themselves, or it proves impossible to avoid a partial release of anxiety, which in turn sets in motion the mechanism of phobia formation. The ideational content of the drive representative is completely removed from consciousness; as a substitute formation and, at the same time, a symptom, there occurs an excessive – in classic cases, somatic – innervation, sometimes a sensory, sometimes a motor innervation, either as an excitation or an inhibition. On closer inspection, the site of the over-innervation proves to be an element of the repressed drive representative itself, which, as if by *condensation*, has drawn the whole energy investment on to itself. Again, of course, these remarks do not explain the whole mechanism of a conversion hysteria; above all, we would need to include the factor of *regression*, which we shall examine in another context.

In that it is made possible only by extensive substitute formations, the repression in hysteria can be judged a complete failure; but as far as dealing with the emotive charge is concerned, the actual task of repression, it is generally a complete success. The process of repression in conversion hysteria terminates with the formation of the symptom and does not have to proceed to a second phase – actually, an unlimited number – as it does in anxiety hysteria.

Repression once again takes an entirely different form in the third disorder we shall draw into this comparison – *compulsion neurosis*. Here we are initially in doubt as to whether the representative under repression is a libidinal or a hostile urge. The uncertainty stems from the fact that compulsion neurosis is based on a regression via which an affectionate impulse is supplanted by a sadistic one. It is this hostile impulse towards a loved person that undergoes repression. The initial effect of the work of repression is very different from its subsequent outcome. At first, it is a complete success – the ideational content is repelled and the emotion made to disappear. As a substitute formation, there occurs an alteration to the ego, a heightened conscientiousness, which can hardly be called a symptom. Here substitute formation and symptom formation diverge. We also learn something about the mechanism of repression here. As always, this has brought about a withdrawal of libido, but it has achieved this by means of a *reaction formation*, by intensifying an opposite. So here the substitute formation has the same mechanism as the repression and, fundamentally, coincides with it, whereas it is both temporally and conceptually distinct from the symptom formation. It is highly likely that the whole process is made possible by the ambivalent relationship into which the sadistic impulse destined for repression has been incorporated.

The initially effective repression cannot, however, endure, and its failure subsequently becomes increasingly apparent. The ambivalence that allowed the repression by reaction formation to take place is also the site where the repressed achieves its return. The emotion that had disappeared re-emerges, transformed into social anxiety, tormented conscience, and unrelenting self-reproach, while the rejected idea undergoes a *substitution by displacement*, often on to something trivial or indifferent. Generally, there is an unmistakable tendency to restore the repressed idea in its entirety. The failure to repress the quantitative, emotive element brings into play the same mechanism of flight by avoidances and prohibitions that we encountered in the formation of hysterical phobias. The rejection of the idea from the conscious is, however, obstinately maintained, because it is this that ensures the check on action, the motor restraint on the impulse. In compulsion neurosis, then, the work of repression ends up in a futile and interminable struggle.

The brief series of comparisons presented here is enough to convince us that more comprehensive investigations are needed before we can hope to fathom the processes involved in repression and neurotic symptom formation. The extraordinary convolutedness of all the factors to be taken into account leaves us with only one means of exposition. We have to approach the material first from one angle, then from another, and so on, each time following this through for as long as it seems to produce results. Each individual approach will, in itself, remain incomplete and will run into obscurities wherever it touches on material we have yet to elaborate; still, we may hope the final synthesis will provide us with a better understanding.

(1915)

Note

1. This useful analogy for the process of repression can also be extended to include a characteristic of repression mentioned earlier. I just need to add that I also have to put a permanent guard on the door that I have forbidden the guest to enter, otherwise he would force it open. (See above.)

The Unconscious

We have learnt from psychoanalysis that the process of repression essentially consists in the idea representing a drive being not removed or destroyed, but prevented from becoming conscious. We say then that it exists in an 'unconscious' state and we have strong evidence that it also remains unconsciously active, even in ways that ultimately reach consciousness. Everything repressed has to remain unconscious, but let us state from the very outset that the repressed does not constitute the whole of the unconscious. The unconscious is the more extensive; the repressed is one part of the unconscious.

How are we to acquire knowledge about the unconscious? We know it, of course, only after it has been transformed or translated into something conscious. Psychoanalytical work provides evidence on a daily basis that this kind of translation is possible. Here the person being analysed is required to overcome certain resistances – the very ones that caused the material to become repressed in the first place by turning it away from the conscious.

1 *In Defence of the Unconscious*

Our right to postulate an unconscious in the psyche, and to use this postulation in scientific work, is contested from many sides. In response, we can state that it is both *necessary* and *legitimate* to postulate the unconscious, and that we have a great deal of *evidence* for its existence. It is necessary because the information provided by consciousness is riddled with gaps; in healthy and sick people alike, psychic acts frequently take place that we can explain only by presupposing other acts that are not registered by consciousness. These include not only 'slips' and dreams in healthy people and everything we call psychic symptoms and compulsions in sick people, but also in our most personal daily experience we encounter ideas of unknown origin and the results of thought processes whose workings remain hidden from us. All of these conscious acts remain incoherent and incomprehensible if we insist that everything occurring in our psyche must also be experienced through consciousness, whereas they fall into demonstrable patterns if we interpolate unconscious acts that we have inferred. We are perfectly justified in going beyond our immediate observations to achieve meaningful connections such as these. When it further transpires that we can base a successful procedure on the postulation of an unconscious, by means of which we can purposefully influence the course of conscious processes, this success provides us with irrefutable evidence that what we have postulated actually exists. We then have to take the view that it is nothing less than an *untenable presumption* to insist that everything occurring in the psyche must also be known to consciousness.

We can go further in support of unconscious psychic states and point out that, at any given moment, only very little is contained in consciousness, so most of what we call conscious knowledge must, in any case, exist for prolonged periods in a state of latency – that is, of psychic unconsciousness. When we take all our latent memories into account, it becomes totally incomprehensible how anyone can deny the existence of the unconscious. Then, however, we meet with the objection that these latent memories can no longer be classed as psychic, but correspond to remnants of somatic processes, from which psychic processes can then re-emerge. The obvious response to this is that, on the contrary, a latent memory is unquestionably the trace of a psychic process. But it is more important to realize that this objection is based on an – unspoken but a priori – equation of the conscious with the psychic. This equation is either a *petitio principii*, which begs the question of whether everything psychic is also necessarily conscious, or it is a matter of convention, of nomenclature. If it is the latter, then of course, like all conventions, it is unfalsifiable. There just remains the question of whether it is so expedient that we have to conform to it. Our answer to this is that the conventional equation of the psychic with the conscious is thoroughly inexpedient. It fractures continuities in the psyche, plunges us into the intractable problems of psycho-physical parallelism, lays itself open to the charge of overestimating the role of consciousness for no apparent reason, and forces us to withdraw prematurely from the field of psychological investigation while bringing no recompense from any other field.

It is clear in any event that the question of whether the – undeniable – latent states in psychic life should be conceived of as physical or unconsciously psychic threatens to end up in a dispute over words. We would be well advised, therefore, to concentrate on what is known for certain about the nature of these problematical states. As far as their physical characteristics are concerned, they are totally inaccessible to us; no physiological concept, no chemical process can give us any notion of their essential nature. On the other hand, it is an established fact that they have very extensive points of contact with conscious psychic processes; they can, with a certain amount of work, be transformed into or replaced by these latter, and they can be described using all the categories we apply to conscious psychic acts, such as ideas, aspirations, resolutions, and so on. Indeed, we have to say of some of these latent states that the only way they differ from conscious ones is precisely in their not being conscious. We shall have no hesitation, then, in treating them as objects of psychological investigation intimately related to conscious psychic acts.

The stubborn refusal to accept that latent acts are psychic in nature can be explained by the fact that most of the phenomena in question have never been studied outside psychoanalysis. Those who are ignorant of pathological facts, who accept that the 'slips' of normal people are accidental, who are content with the old saying *'Träume sind Schäume'* ('dreams are froth') need ignore only a few more riddles of the psychology of consciousness to spare themselves the trouble of postulating unconscious psychic activity. Incidentally, even in the days before psychoanalysis, hypnotic experiments, especially post-hypnotic suggestion, provided concrete demonstrations of the existence and mode of operation of the psychic unconscious.

To postulate an unconscious is also entirely *legitimate* in that, by doing so, we do not depart in the slightest from our customary way of thinking, widely held to be correct. Consciousness informs each of us only about our own psychic states; that other people also have a consciousness is something we infer by analogy from their observable utterances and actions in order to make sense of their behaviour. (No doubt it would be psychologically more correct to say we attribute our own constitution, and therefore our consciousness, to everyone else outside us without really thinking about it, and this identification is a prerequisite of our understanding.) At one time our ego extended this inference – or identification – to other people, animals, plants, inanimate objects, indeed the whole world, and where there was an overwhelming similarity with the individual ego, it proved useful, though it became proportionately less reliable, the greater the difference between the self and the other entity. Nowadays, our critical judgement is uncertain even about animal consciousness, refuses to accept plant consciousness, and relegates the notion that inanimate objects have consciousness to mysticism. But even where our primal tendency towards identification withstands critical scrutiny – with respect to our fellow human beings – this assumption of a consciousness is still based on an inference and can never share the immediate certainty we have of our own consciousness.

Psychoanalysis asks nothing more than that we also apply this process of deduction to our own person, though, admittedly, we have no constitutional tendency to do so. If we proceed in this way, we have to say that all the actions and expressions we can observe in ourselves and cannot relate to the rest of our psychic life must be judged as if they belonged to another person, and must be explained in terms of a psychic life ascribed to that person. Experience does indeed show that we know perfectly well how to interpret, i.e., assimilate into a psychic context, the very same acts in other people that we refuse to acknowledge in our own psyche. Here some obstacle evidently deflects our investigations away from our own person, preventing us from proper self-knowledge.

This process of deduction – applied to our own person despite inner resistance – leads not to the discovery of an unconscious, but, strictly speaking, to the postulation of another, second consciousness within us, married to the one we already know. This, however, prompts some legitimate criticisms. First, a consciousness unknown to its own bearer is something quite different from another person's consciousness, indeed it is questionable whether such a consciousness – devoid of its own most important characteristic – even merits further discussion at all. Anyone rejecting the postulation of a psychic unconscious will certainly not be content to accept an *unconscious consciousness* in its place. Second, analysis shows that the various latent psychic processes we infer enjoy a great degree of mutual independence, as if they stood in no relation to and knew nothing of each other. We would therefore need to be prepared to postulate not only a second consciousness within us, but also a third, fourth, perhaps an unlimited series of states of consciousness, all unknown both to ourselves and to each other. Third, and the most substantial argument of all to be taken into consideration, analytical research reveals that some of these latent processes have characteristics and peculiarities that appear alien, even incredible, to us, and stand in complete contrast to the known attributes of consciousness. We have good reason, then, to revise our deduction regarding our own person: what we have within us is not a second consciousness, but psychic acts that are devoid of consciousness. We can also reject the term 'subconsciousness' as incorrect and misleading. The known cases of *'double conscience'* (split consciousness) do not contradict our theory. They can most accurately be described as cases of a splitting of psychic activity into two groups, with the same consciousness alternating between the two sites.

In psychoanalysis we have no choice but to insist that psychic processes are in themselves unconscious, and the way they are perceived by consciousness is comparable to the way the outside world is perceived by the sense organs. This analogy might even provide us with some new insights. The psychoanalytical postulation of unconscious psychic activity seems, on the one hand, to be a further continuation of the primitive animism that once surrounded us with reflections of our own consciousness, and on the other, to be an extension of Kant's revision of the way we conceive of external perception. Just as Kant warned us against overlooking how our perception is subjectively determined and cannot be regarded as identical to the unknowable thing that is perceived, so psychoanalysis warns us not to mistake our perceptions of consciousness for the unconscious psychic processes that are their object. As with the physical world, psychic life need not, in reality, be how it appears to us. Fortunately, though, we can expect the revision of internal perception to present fewer difficulties than that of external perception, the inner object being less unknowable than the outside world.

II The Ambiguity of the Term 'Unconscious' and the Topographical Perspective

Before we go any further, let us state the important, though troublesome, fact that unconsciousness is just one attribute of psychic material, one which by no means sufficiently characterizes it. There are psychic acts widely varying in status that nevertheless share this characteristic of being unconscious. The unconscious comprises, on the one hand, acts that are merely latent, temporarily unconscious but otherwise no different from conscious ones, and, on the other, processes such as repressed ones, which, if they were to become conscious, would contrast starkly with the other conscious ones. It would put an end to any misunderstandings if, when describing the various kinds of psychic acts from now on, we were to disregard whether they were conscious or unconscious and to classify and correlate them solely in terms of their relation to drives and aims, their composition, and their location in the hierarchy of psychic systems. For various reasons, though, this is impracticable, so we cannot avoid the ambiguity of using the words conscious and unconscious sometimes in the descriptive sense, sometimes in the systematic sense, the latter signifying their belonging to a specific system and their possession of certain characteristics. We could try to avoid this confusion by giving the psychic systems we have identified arbitrarily chosen names, which make no reference to consciousness. Beforehand, though, we would need to specify on what basis we are differentiating between the systems, and here we would not be able to evade the issue of consciousness as this forms the starting-point of all our investigations. It might be of some help if, when using the two words in the systematic sense, we substitute, at least in writing, the designation *cs* for consciousness and the corresponding abbreviation *ucs* for the unconscious.

Moving on to a positive account of psychoanalytical findings, we can state that a psychic act generally goes through two phases, between which is interposed a kind of inspection (*censorship*). In the first phase the act is unconscious and belongs to the *ucs* system. If, on being inspected, it is rejected by the censorship, it is not allowed to proceed to the second phase; it is then said to be 'repressed' and has to remain unconscious. If, however, it passes this inspection, it enters the second phase and becomes part of the second system we are calling the *cs*. The fact that it belongs to this system does not, however, definitively determine its relationship to consciousness. It is still not conscious, though it certainly is *capable of consciousness* (to use J. Breuer's expression), i.e., certain conditions being met, it can now become an object of consciousness without any particular resistance. In view of this capacity for consciousness, we also call the *cs* system the *'preconscious'*. If it should emerge that some form of censorship is also involved in determining whether the preconscious becomes conscious, we shall sharpen our distinction between the *pcs* and *cs* systems. For the time being, it suffices to say that the *pcs* system shares the same qualities as the *cs* system, and the strict censorship is carried out at the point of transition from the *ucs* to the *pcs* (or *cs*).

By adopting these (two or three) psychic systems, psychoanalysis takes a further step away from the purely descriptive psychology of consciousness and provides itself with a new set of questions and a new content. Until now, it has distinguished itself from this psychology mainly by virtue of its *dynamic* view of psychic processes; now it also seeks to take into account the *topography* of the psyche and to determine in which system or between which systems any given psychic act takes place. This endeavour has also led to it being called *depth psychology*. Later we shall hear that it can be further supplemented by a third perspective.

If we are serious about producing a topography of psychic acts, we must turn our attention to a question arising at this point. When a psychic act (let us confine ourselves here to one in the nature of an idea) is transferred from the *ucs* system to the *cs* (or *pcs*) system, are we to assume this transfer involves a new registration – a second inscription, so to speak – of the idea in question, which might therefore also be situated in a new psychic locality, with the original unconscious inscription continuing to exist alongside it? Or are we to suppose the transfer consists in a change in state, involving the same material at the same locality? This may seem an abstruse question, but it is one we must ask if we hope to form a more definite idea of psychic topography, of the psychic dimension of depth. It is a difficult question because it goes beyond the purely psychological and touches on the relations between the psychic apparatus and anatomy. We know, very roughly speaking, that such relations do exist. Research has provided indisputable proof that psychic activity is bound up with the functioning of the brain as with no other organ. We are then taken further – how far exactly, we do not know – by the discovery that the various parts of the brain differ in status and have special relationships with specific parts of the body or mental functions. But every attempt to go on and hypothesize a localization of psychic processes, every endeavour to conceive of ideas as something stored in nerve cells, or excitations as something travelling along nerve fibres, has been a complete failure. The same fate would await any theory that attempted to identify, say, the anatomical location of the *cs* system – conscious psychic activity – in the cerebral cortex, or to locate unconscious processes in the subcortical areas of the brain. There is a yawning gap here that cannot possibly be filled at present, nor is this the task of psychology. *Provisionally*, our psychic topography has nothing to do with anatomy; it refers not to anatomical localities, but to regions in the psychic apparatus, wherever these may be situated in the body.

In this respect, then, our work is independent and can proceed according to its own requirements. It will also be useful to remind ourselves that, initially, our hypotheses can lay claim only to the status of graphic illustrations. The first of the two possibilities considered above – that the *cs* phase of an idea involves a new inscription of it at a different location – is without doubt the cruder, but also the more convenient. The second assumption – that of a merely *functional* change of state – is initially the more probable, but it is less concrete, less easy to work with. The first, topographical, assumption implies a topographical separation of the *ucs* and *cs* systems, and the possibility of an idea being present in two places at once in the psychic apparatus – even regularly moving, if unimpeded by censorship, from one place to the other, perhaps without the first location or inscription being lost. This may seem strange, but it is supported by observations made during psychoanalytical practice.

When we inform a patient of an idea he has at one time repressed and which we have deduced, this does not, at first, alter his psychic state in any way. Above all, it neither lifts the repression nor undoes its effects, as we might perhaps have expected since the previously unconscious idea has now become conscious. On the contrary, we initially achieve only a renewed rejection of the repressed idea. Now, though, the patient really does have the same idea in two forms at different locations in his psychic apparatus; first, he has the conscious memory of the auditory trace of the idea as related by the analyst; second, alongside this, he has within himself – as we know for certain – the unconscious memory of the experience in its original form. The repression is not actually lifted until we overcome the resistances and bring the conscious idea into connection with the unconscious memory trace. The only way to achieve this is to make the memory trace itself conscious. Viewed superficially, this might seem to prove that conscious and unconscious ideas are separate, topographically distinct inscriptions of the same content. But a moment's further reflection tells us that there is only an apparent identity between the analyst's communication and the patient's repressed memory. Having heard something and having experienced it are, in their psychological nature, two very different things, even when they have the same content.

Initially, then, we are not in a position to decide between the two possibilities under consideration. Perhaps later we shall come across factors that can tip the balance in favour of one or the other. Or perhaps we shall discover that the question itself is inadequate and that the distinction between unconscious and conscious ideas needs to be defined in a totally different way.

III *Unconscious Feelings*

Having restricted the above discussion to ideas, we can now ask a new question, the answer to which can only help clarify our theoretical views. We have said there are conscious and unconscious ideas, but are there also unconscious drive impulses, feelings, sensations, and so on, or are such composite terms meaningless here?

I do indeed think the opposition of conscious and unconscious does not apply to drives. A drive can never be an object of consciousness, only the idea representing it. But even in the unconscious it can be represented only by this idea. If drives were not attached to ideas and did not manifest themselves as emotional states, we could know nothing of them. When we do speak of an unconscious or repressed drive impulse, this is a harmless laxity of expression. We can mean only a drive impulse whose ideational representative is unconscious, for no other possibility exists.

We might think it would be just as easy to settle the question of unconscious sensations, feelings and emotions. After all, it belongs to the very essence of a feeling that it is felt – i.e., known to consciousness. It would be quite impossible, then, for feelings, sensations and emotions to be unconscious. In psychoanalytical practice, however, we regularly speak of unconscious love, hate, anger, etc., and we even find we cannot avoid the strange combination 'unconscious sense of guilt' or the paradoxical 'unconscious anxiety'. Do we mean something more by these expressions than when we speak of 'unconscious drives'?

It is indeed a different state of affairs here. First, it can happen that an emotional impulse is perceived but misconstrued. Due to its own representative being repressed, it is forced to attach itself to another idea, and it is then regarded by consciousness as an expression of that idea. When we restore the true context, we call the original emotional impulse 'unconscious', even though its emotion was never unconscious, only the idea representing it had succumbed to repression. The expressions 'unconscious emotion' and 'unconscious feeling' refer, in general, to the fate experienced, as a consequence of repression, by the quantitative factor of the drive impulse. We know this fate can be one of three things: either the emotion remains, wholly or in part, as it is; or it is transformed into a qualitatively different emotional charge, usually anxiety; or it is suppressed, i.e., prevented from developing at all. (These different possibilities can be studied in dream-work perhaps even more easily than in the neuroses.) We also know that the actual aim of repression is to suppress the development of emotion, and its work is not complete until this aim is achieved. Wherever repression succeeds in inhibiting the development of emotion, we call any emotion we restore by undoing the work of repression 'unconscious'. It cannot be disputed, then, that this use of language is logically consistent, but in comparison with unconscious ideas there is a significant difference in that, after repression, an unconscious idea continues to exist as an actual structure in the *ucs* system, whereas an unconscious emotion here represents only a potential onset that has been prevented from developing. Strictly speaking, then, although the expression is not wrong, unconscious emotions do not exist in the same way as unconscious ideas. Nevertheless, emotional formations, which become conscious like any other, certainly can exist in the *ucs* system. The difference stems entirely from the fact that ideas are investments of energy – basically in memory traces – whereas emotions and feelings correspond to processes of discharge whose ultimate expressions are perceived as sensations. The present state of our knowledge of emotions and feelings does not allow us to formulate this difference any more clearly.

That repression can succeed in inhibiting the transformation of a drive impulse into expressions of emotion is particularly interesting to us. It shows that the *cs* system normally controls emotionality as well as access to motility, and it elevates the significance of repression by revealing it to be capable of withholding something not only from consciousness, but also from emotional development and muscle activation. Conversely, we can say that as long as the *cs* system controls emotionality and motility, the psychic state of that individual can be described as normal. Nevertheless, there is an unmistakable difference in the relation of the ruling system to these two closely related discharge processes.[1] Whereas the control of the *cs* over voluntary motility is firmly established, regularly withstanding the onslaught of neurosis and breaking down only in psychosis, its control over the development of emotion is less secure. Even within normal life we witness a constant struggle between the *cs* and *ucs* systems for primacy over emotionality, with certain spheres of influence being marked off from each other and fusions occurring between the forces at work.

The significance of the *cs* (*pcs*) system in controlling access to releases of emotion and action also allows us to understand the role played by substitute ideas in determining the form illnesses take. It is possible for the development of emotion to proceed directly from the *ucs* system, in which case it always has the character of anxiety, for which all 'repressed' emotions are exchanged. Often, though, the drive impulse has to wait until it has found a substitute idea in the *cs* system. The development of emotion is then facilitated by this conscious substitute, the qualitative character of the emotion being determined by the nature of the idea. We claimed that repression involves a dissociation of the emotion from the idea to which it belongs, with each going on to experience a separate fate. As a description, this cannot be disputed; as a rule, though, the actual process is that the emotion cannot come about until it has succeeded in breaking through to a new form of representation in the *cs* system.

Note

1. Emotionality essentially manifests itself in motor (secretory, vasomotor) discharges that alter the subject's own body (internally) with no reference to the outside world, whereas motility manifests itself in actions intended to alter the outside world.

IV *The Topography and Dynamics of Repression*

We came to the conclusion that repression is essentially a process affecting ideas on the border between the *ucs* and *pcs* (*cs*) systems, and we can now renew our attempt to describe this process in more detail. It must involve a *withdrawal* of investment, but the question is, in which system does this withdrawal take place, and to which system does the withdrawn investment belong?

A repressed idea remains capable of action in the *ucs*, so it must have retained its investment and it must be something else that has been withdrawn. If we take the case of actual (follow-up) repression as it affects a preconscious, or even already conscious idea, this repression can consist only in the withdrawal from the idea of the (pre)conscious investment, belonging to the *pcs* system. Then the idea either remains uninvested, or it is invested with energy from the *ucs*, or it retains the *ucs* investment it already had. So: withdrawal of the preconscious investment, retention of the unconscious investment, or replacement of the preconscious with an unconscious investment. Note, incidentally, how we have almost inadvertently based these reflections on the assumption that the transition from the *ucs* to the next system occurs via not a new inscription, but a change in state – a transformation of the investment. In this instance the functional hypothesis has easily ousted the topographical one.

This process of libido withdrawal is not, however, sufficient to explain another characteristic of repression. It is not clear why the idea, which remains invested with energy or receives a new supply from the *ucs*, does not use this investment to renew its attempt to break into the *pcs* system. Then the withdrawal of libido would have to be repeated, and the same procedure would continue indefinitely, although the outcome would not be that of repression. Equally, the above mechanism – withdrawal of the preconscious investment – fails to account for primal repression; here we have an unconscious idea that has not yet been invested from the *pcs*, so it cannot have this investment withdrawn.

What is required here, then, is another process, which in the first case maintains the repression and in the second is responsible both for establishing and continuing it. For this we need to postulate a *counterinvestment*, by means of which the *pcs* system protects itself against the pressure of the unconscious idea. Examples taken from clinical practice can show how these counterinvestments, which occur in the *pcs* system, manifest themselves. It is the counterinvestment that represents the ongoing expenditure in primal repression, and which also guarantees the durability of the repression. In primal repression it is the sole mechanism, whereas in actual (follow-up) repression it is accompanied by the withdrawal of the *pcs* investment. It may very well be that it is precisely this energy withdrawn from the idea that is used to create the counterinvestment.

We see how we have gradually come to introduce a third perspective into our account of psychic phenomena: in addition to the dynamic and topographical perspectives, the *economic* perspective, which seeks to trace the fates of the quantities of excitation and to estimate their size, at least in relative terms. It would not be unreasonable to distinguish this overall perspective – the culmination of all psychoanalytical investigation – with its own special name. When we succeed in describing a psychic process in its *dynamic*, *topographical* and *economic* aspects, I propose we call this a *metapsychological* account. Given the present state of our knowledge, we can safely say this will prove possible only in a few isolated areas.

Let us tentatively try to describe in metapsychological terms the process of repression in the three known transference neuroses. Here we may substitute the term 'libido' for 'investment', because, as we know, we are dealing with the fates of sexual drives.

In anxiety hysteria a preliminary phase of the process is often overlooked, and perhaps actually skipped over, too, but on careful observation it can be easily recognized. It consists in anxiety occurring with no apparent object. We presume a love impulse was present in the *ucs* demanding to be transferred into the *pcs* system; but, as a kind of attempt at flight, the investment directed towards it from the *pcs* was withdrawn and the unconscious libidinal investment of the rejected idea was discharged as anxiety. During some subsequent repetition of this process, a first step was then taken towards mastering this undesirable development of anxiety. The fleeing investment attached itself to a substitute idea, which, on the one hand, was related by association to the rejected idea and, on the other, was sufficiently remote from it to escape repression (*substitution by displacement*), allowing the still uninhibitable development of anxiety to be rationalized. The substitute idea then acts as a counterinvestment in the *cs* (*pcs*) system, guarding against any recurrence of the repressed idea in the *cs*; on the other hand, it is, or acts as if it were, the source of the release of anxiety, which is now more uninhibitable than ever. Clinical observation reveals, for example, that a child suffering from an animal phobia experiences anxiety in two situations, first when the repressed love impulse becomes intensified, second when he perceives the feared animal. In the first instance the substitute idea acts as a point of transition from the *ucs* to the *cs* system, in the second as an independent source of anxiety. The *cs* system tends to manifest its increasing dominance through the substitute idea increasingly being stimulated in the second rather than the first way. The child may ultimately behave as if it felt no affection at all towards its father, having freed itself from him entirely, and as if it really were afraid of the animal. But this fear of the animal – fed, as it is, from the unconscious drive source – proves so stubborn and excessive in the face of all influence from the *cs* system that it betrays its origins in the *ucs* system.

In the second phase of anxiety hysteria, then, the counterinvestment from the *cs* system leads to a substitute formation. The same mechanism soon finds itself brought into play once again. As we know, the process of repression is not yet complete, and it takes on the new task of inhibiting the anxiety provoked by the substitute.

This is achieved by the whole network of associations surrounding the substitute idea being invested with particular intensity, making it extremely sensitive to excitation. Due to its association with the substitute idea, excitation of any part of this surrounding structure inevitably gives rise to a slight development of anxiety, which then functions as a signal to inhibit any further development of the anxiety by repeating the flight of the investment. The further these sensitive and alert counterinvestments extend around the feared substitute, the more effectively the mechanism to isolate the substitute idea and prevent further excitations of it functions. Of course, these precautions guard only against excitations of the substitute idea coming from outside, through perception, never against the drive impulse, which affects the substitute idea on account of its association with the repressed idea. They begin to work, then, only when the substitute has fully taken over representation of the repressed idea, and they are never completely reliable. With every increase in drive excitation, the protective ramparts around the substitute idea must extend themselves a little further outwards. The whole construction, which is produced in analogous ways in the other neuroses, is termed a *phobia*. The flight from conscious investment of the substitute idea manifests itself in the avoidances, renunciations and prohibitions characteristic of anxiety hysteria. If we survey the process as a whole, we can say the third phase repeats the work of the second on a larger scale. The *cs* system now protects itself against activation of the substitute idea by counterinvesting the area surrounding it, just as previously it had secured itself against the emergence of the repressed idea by investing the substitute idea. The process of substitute formation by displacement is thus continued. We should also add that previously the *cs* system had only one small point of entry at which the repressed drive impulse could break through, namely the substitute idea, but ultimately the whole phobic construction becomes just such an enclave of unconscious influence. Furthermore, we can emphasize the interesting point that this defence process as a whole brings about a projection outwards of the danger from the drive. The ego behaves as if it were in danger of a development of anxiety caused not by a drive impulse, but by a perception, allowing it to react to this external danger with attempts at flight, namely the phobic avoidances. In this process, repression at least succeeds in stemming the release of anxiety to a certain extent, but only at a heavy sacrifice of personal freedom. Nevertheless, attempts at flight from drive demands are, in general, futile, and the phobic flight ultimately remains unsatisfactory.

Much of what we have ascertained about the circumstances in anxiety hysteria also holds true for the other two neuroses, so we can confine our discussion to the various points of difference and the role played by counterinvestment. In conversion hysteria, the investment of drive energy in the repressed idea is transformed into innervation of the symptom. To what extent and under what circumstances the unconscious idea is drained of energy by this discharge into innervation sufficiently to cause it to relinquish its pressure on the *cs* system – these and similar questions are best reserved for a special investigation into hysteria. The role played in conversion hysteria by the counterinvestment from the *cs* (*pcs*) system is clear and manifests itself in the symptom formation. It is the counterinvestment that selects the one element of the drive representative on which the whole of its investment can be concentrated. The element selected to be the symptom must fulfil the condition of giving expression to the wishful aim of the drive impulse no less than to the defensive or punitive endeavours of the *cs* system; it is overinvested, then, and maintained from both directions, just like the substitute idea in anxiety hysteria. We can easily conclude from this that the amount of energy expended on repression by the *cs* system does not need to be as great as the energy invested in the symptom; this is because the intensity of the repression is measured by the expenditure on counterinvestment, whereas the symptom is maintained both by this counterinvestment and by the drive investment from the *ucs* system that it also has condensed within it.

As for compulsion neurosis, all we would need to add to the account in the previous essay is that here the counterinvestment from the *cs* system comes most prominently to the fore. It is the counterinvestment, organized as a reaction formation, which brings about the initial repression, and this counterinvestment is also the point at which the repressed idea subsequently manages to break through. We may venture to suppose that it is the prominence of the counterinvestment and the absence of a discharge outlet that make the repression seem so much less successful in anxiety hysteria and compulsion neurosis than in conversion hysteria.

v *The Special Properties of the* Ucs *System*

The distinction between the two psychic systems takes on new significance when we observe that the processes in one system, the *ucs*, display properties not found in the system immediately above it.

The core of the *ucs* consists of drive representatives seeking to discharge their investment, in other words, wish impulses. These drive impulses are not subordinate to each other, they exist side by side without being influenced by each other, and they do not contradict each other. When two wish impulses with apparently incompatible aims are activated simultaneously, they do not detract from each other, say, or cancel each other out, but instead join forces to form an intermediate aim, a compromise.

In this system there is no negation, no doubt, no sliding scale of certainty – all of these are first introduced by the work of the censorship between the *ucs* and the *pcs*. Negation is a substitute for repression at a higher level. In the *ucs* there are only contents that are more or less strongly invested.

The intensities of investment energy are much more mobile here. By the process of *displacement*, an idea can transfer the whole charge of its investment to another idea, or, by the process of *condensation*, take on the whole investment of several others. I have suggested that we regard these two mechanisms as indicative of so-called *primary processes*. In the *pcs* system *secondary processes* predominate;[1] when elements from the *pcs* system are subjected to a primary process, the effect is 'comic' and provokes laughter.

Processes in the *ucs* system are *timeless*, i.e., are not chronologically ordered, are not altered by the passage of time, indeed bear no relation to time whatsoever. Temporal relations, too, are bound up with the work of the *cs* system.

Ucs processes pay equally little heed to *reality*. They are subject to the pleasure principle; their fate depends only on how strong they are and whether they meet the requirements of pleasure–unpleasure regulation.

In summary, the characteristics we can expect to find in the processes belonging to the *ucs* system are: *absence of contradiction, the primary process* (mobility of investments), *timelessness* and *substitution of psychic reality for external reality.*[2]

Unconscious processes are discernible to us only under the conditions of dreaming and neurosis, that is, when the processes of the higher *pcs* system revert to an earlier, lower stage (regression). In themselves, they are unknowable, indeed not even capable of existing, because very early on the *ucs* system is overlaid by the *pcs*, which has usurped access to consciousness and motility. The *ucs* system discharges its energy into the physical innervations that correspond to the development of emotions, but, as we have heard, even this discharge outlet is contested by the *pcs*. Under normal circumstances, the *ucs* system could not, by itself, carry out purposive muscle actions, with the exception of those already organized as reflexes.

We can appreciate the full significance of the characteristics of the *ucs* system, described above, only by comparing and contrasting them with the properties of the *pcs* system. But this would involve such a major digression that I suggest we once again declare a postponement until we can carry out this comparison in the context of an appraisal of the higher system. For now, we need mention only the most salient points.

Processes in the *pcs* system – regardless of whether they are already conscious or merely capable of consciousness – demonstrate an inhibition of the tendency of invested ideas towards discharge. When a process passes from one idea to another, the first idea retains part of its investment, with only a small proportion of it being displaced. Displacements and condensations such as occur in primary processes are excluded or heavily restricted. This circumstance has led J. Breuer to postulate two distinct states of investment energy in psychic life, one tonically fixed, the other freely mobile and striving for discharge. I believe this distinction represents our most profound insight yet into the nature of nervous energy, and I see no way around it. A metapsychological account would, as a matter of priority, need to continue the discussion at this point, but perhaps that would, as yet, be too bold an undertaking.

The *pcs* system is also responsible for making interaction possible between ideational contents so that they can influence one another, for ordering these ideas chronologically, for introducing one or more forms of censorship, for reality-testing, and for the reality principle. Conscious memory, too, seems to be totally dependent on the *pcs*. This should be clearly distinguished from memory traces – in which the experiences of the *ucs* are fixed – and probably corresponds to a special kind of inscription, such as we tried, before rejecting it, to postulate for the relationship between conscious and unconscious ideas. It is in this connection, too, that we shall find a way of putting an end to our vacillation in naming this higher system, which at the moment we randomly call *pcs* one minute, *cs* the next.

Here would also be the place to warn against making premature generalizations about what we have brought to light concerning the division of psychic functions between the two systems. We are describing the situation as exhibited in the mature adult, in whom, strictly speaking, the *ucs* system functions only as a preliminary stage of the higher organization. What contents and relations this system has over the course of individual development – and what significance it has in animals – should be investigated independently, not inferred from our description. And in human beings we should be prepared to find pathological conditions, say, in which the two systems modify and even swap their contents and their characteristics.

Notes

1. See the discussion in Chapter VII of *The Interpretation of Dreams*, based on ideas developed by J. Breuer in *Studies on Hysteria*.
2. We shall refer to another significant privilege of the *ucs* later, in a different context.

VI *Interaction between the Two Systems*

It would certainly be wrong to imagine that the *ucs* remains at rest while all the psychic work is done by the *pcs*, or that the *ucs* is something discarded, a vestigial organ or a leftover from evolution. It would be equally wrong to assume that interaction between the two systems is confined to the act of repression, with the *pcs* casting everything it finds disturbing into the abyss of the *ucs*. On the contrary, the *ucs* is a living thing capable of development, and it maintains a number of other relations with the *pcs*, including co-operation. In short, we must say that the *ucs* remains active through its so-called derivatives, that it is open to influences from life, and that it constantly influences – and, conversely, is even subject to influences from – the *pcs*.

Studying the derivatives of the *ucs* will thoroughly dash any expectations we have of a schematically clear-cut distinction between the two systems. No doubt this will cause our findings to be deemed unsatisfactory and will probably be used to cast doubt on the value of the way we differentiate between the psychic processes. We shall, however, insist that our only task is to translate the results of our observations into theory, and reject any obligation to produce, at our first attempt, a polished and cogently simple theory. We shall stand by the complexities of our theory as long as they prove relevant to our observations, and we shall continue to hope that precisely these complexities will ultimately lead us to discover facts that, though simple in themselves, can do justice to the complexities of reality.

Among the derivatives of *ucs* drive impulses of the character described above, there are some that simultaneously have diametrically opposed attributes. On the one hand, they are highly organized and free from contradiction, have taken advantage of all the acquisitions of the *cs* system, and would be hard to tell apart from the formations in this system. On the other hand, they are unconscious and incapable of consciousness. Qualitatively, then, they belong to the *pcs* system, but in actuality they belong to the *ucs*, and this origin remains the decisive factor in determining their fate. We can compare them to people of mixed race who largely resemble whites but who betray their coloured descent by some or other prominent trait and therefore remain excluded from society, enjoying none of the privileges of white people. Examples include the fantasy formations of both healthy and neurotic people, which we recognize as preliminary stages in dream and symptom formation, and which, despite their high degree of organization, remain repressed and therefore incapable of consciousness. They can approach consciousness and remain undisturbed provided they are not strongly invested, but as soon as they cross a certain threshold of investment, they are driven back. Substitute formations are similar such highly organized derivatives of the *ucs*, although these can succeed in breaking through into consciousness if the circumstances are favourable – for example, if they can align themselves with a counterinvestment in the *pcs*.

Some of the difficulties arising here will be resolved when, elsewhere, we investigate more thoroughly the preconditions of the act of becoming conscious. It might be useful at this point to contrast our approach so far – from the *ucs* upwards – with one proceeding from consciousness. The whole sum of psychic processes presents itself to consciousness as the realm of the preconscious. A very sizeable part of this preconscious stems from the unconscious, has the characteristics of derivatives of the unconscious, and is subject to censorship before it can become conscious. Another part of the *pcs* is capable of consciousness without censorship. Here we find ourselves at variance with an earlier assumption. When looking at repression, we had to locate the censorship determining what can and cannot become conscious between the *ucs* and *pcs* systems. Now it seems there is a censorship between the *pcs* and the *cs*. But we would do well not to see this complication as a difficulty, and instead assume that every transition from one system to the one immediately above it – that is, every advance to a higher stage of psychic organization – involves a new process of censorship. This would, of course, dispense with our hypothesis of a continuous renewal of inscriptions.

We can put all these difficulties down to the fact that consciousness – the only characteristic of psychic processes directly imparted to us – is by no means a suitable criterion for differentiating between the systems. Apart from the fact that the conscious is not always conscious, but at times also latent, observation reveals that much material which shares the characteristics of the *pcs* system never becomes conscious, and later we shall learn that the process of becoming conscious is restricted by certain aspects of the manner in which attention is directed. There is no simple relationship, then, between consciousness and the various systems, nor between consciousness and repression. The truth is that not only the repressed remains alien to consciousness, but also some of the impulses governing our ego, i.e., that which, in terms of function, stands in the starkest possible contrast to the repressed. The further we wish to forge ahead with a metapsychological conception of psychic life, the more we must learn to emancipate ourselves from the significance of the symptom of 'consciousness'.

As long as we remain fixed on this latter, we shall find our generalizations constantly being undermined by exceptions. We see derivatives of the *ucs* becoming conscious as substitute formations and symptoms, the unconscious material generally having been heavily distorted but often retaining many characteristics that normally provoke repression. Equally, we find many preconscious formations remaining unconscious even though their nature is such that we would have expected them to be capable of consciousness. Here the stronger attraction of the *ucs* is probably making itself felt. All of this prompts us to seek the more significant distinction not between the conscious and the preconscious, but between the preconscious and the unconscious. When the *ucs* is turned back by censorship at the border of the *pcs*, derivatives of it can circumvent this censorship, become highly organized, and achieve a certain intensity of investment in the *pcs*; when, however, they cross this threshold of intensity and try to force their way into consciousness, they are recognized as derivatives of the *ucs* and are repressed anew by the censorship at the border between the *pcs* and the *cs*. Thus the first censorship operates on the *ucs* itself, the second on its *pcs* derivatives. It would seem that over the course of individual development the censorship had moved forward a step.

Psychoanalytical practice provides indisputable evidence for the existence of this second censorship between the *pcs* and *cs* systems. We ask the patient to produce a wealth of derivatives of the *ucs* and demand that he overcome the censorship that objects to these preconscious formations becoming conscious, then we use the overthrow of this censorship to pave the way for the removal of the repression brought about by the earlier censorship. We should add here that the existence of this censorship between the *pcs* and the *cs* lets us know that becoming conscious is not merely an act of perception, but probably also an *overinvestment*, a further advance in psychic organization.

Let us now turn to the interaction between the *ucs* and the other systems, not so much to establish any new facts as to avoid overlooking the obvious. At the roots of drive activity the systems communicate with each other most extensively. Some of the processes instigated here pass through the *ucs* as through a preparatory stage and reach their highest psychic development in the *cs*, others are kept back as part of the *ucs*. But experiences stemming from external perception can also impinge on the *ucs*. Normally all paths from perception to the *ucs* remain open; only those leading out of the *ucs* can be blocked by repression.

It is a highly remarkable fact that the *ucs* of one person can act on that of another while bypassing the *cs* completely. This merits more detailed investigation, particularly to see if we can exclude the involvement of preconscious activity; as a described fact, though, it is indisputable.

The content of the *pcs* (or *cs*) system stems partly from the life of the drives (mediated through the *ucs*), partly from perception. It is unclear to what extent the processes in this system can directly influence the *ucs*; research into pathological cases often reveals the *ucs* to have an almost incredible degree of independence and resistance to influence. A complete divergence of the currents, a total disintegration of the two systems, is the basic characteristic of illness. But psychoanalytical treatment is founded on the influence the *cs* can have on the *ucs*, and at least shows that such a thing, although laborious, is not impossible. As we have already said, derivatives of the *ucs*, which mediate between the two systems, pave the way for us here. Nevertheless, we can safely assume that any spontaneous modification of the *ucs* by the *cs* is a slow and difficult process.

Co-operation can occur between a preconscious and an unconscious – even a powerfully repressed – impulse if a situation arises in which the unconscious impulse can work in tandem with one of the ruling impulses. Repression is lifted in this instance and the repressed activity is permitted as a reinforcement of the one intended by the ego. In this one constellation, the unconscious is aligned with the ego without its repression being otherwise modified. The effect of the *ucs* in these collaborations is unmistakable; the reinforced tendencies behave differently from normal ones – they make possible achievements of especial perfection, and they show the same sort of resistance to opposition as any compulsive symptom.

We can compare the content of the *ucs* to a native population in the psyche. If human beings do inherit psychic formations, something analogous to animal instincts, then these are what form the core of the *ucs*. Everything that is discarded over the course of infantile development – material not necessarily different in nature from that which is inherited – is then subsequently added to this core. As a rule, a sharp and definitive distinction between the contents of the two systems does not come about until puberty.

VII *Identifying the Unconscious*

What we have gathered together in the preceding discussions is about as much as can be said about the *ucs* as long as we are drawing only on our knowledge of dream-life and the transference neuroses. It is certainly not much, and in places comes across as obscure and confused; above all, it offers us no scope for correlating or subsuming the *ucs* into any context with which we are already familiar. Only the analysis of one of the disorders we call narcissistic psychoneuroses promises to provide us with the conceptions we need to get closer – within touching distance, as it were – to the enigmatic *ucs*.

Since the publication of a work by Abraham (1908), which the conscientious author attributes to my instigation, we have tried to characterize Kraepelin's dementia praecox (Bleuler's schizophrenia) in terms of its relationship to the opposition between ego and object. There was nothing about the transference neuroses (anxiety hysteria, conversion hysteria, compulsion neurosis) that brought this opposition to the fore. We knew, of course, that the onset of neurosis is triggered by lack of satisfaction from the object, and that neurosis involves renunciation of the real object; we also knew that the libido withdrawn from the real object reverts first to a fantasized object, then to a repressed one (introversion). In these illnesses, though, the object-investment as a whole is vigorously maintained, and a more detailed examination of the process of repression has led us to assume that, in spite of – or rather because of – repression, the object-investment continues to exist in the *ucs* system. In fact, this undisturbed object-investment is a prerequisite of the capacity for transference that we exploit in the treatment of these disorders.

In schizophrenia, on the other hand, we have been compelled to assume that after the process of repression, the withdrawn libido does not seek a new object, but instead retreats into the ego; here, then, the object-investments are abandoned and a primitive objectless state of narcissism is restored. The lack of a capacity for transference in these patients (as far as the pathological process extends), their resulting imperviousness to therapy, their character-istic rejection of the outside world, the appearance of indications of an overinvestment of their own ego, the final outcome of complete apathy – all of these clinical characteristics seem perfectly in keeping with the assumption that object-investments have been abandoned. As for the relationship between the two psychic systems, all observers have been struck by the fact that in schizophrenia a great deal is consciously expressed that in the transference neuroses would require psychoanalysis before being detected in the *ucs*. Initially, though, we were not able to establish any intelligible connection between ego-object relations and the relations of consciousness.

This sought-after connection seems to emerge in the following unexpected way. In schizophrenics – especially in the very revealing early stages – we can observe a number of *linguistic* changes, some of which merit being viewed from a specific perspective. These patients often take particular care over the way they express them-selves, which becomes 'choice' and 'affected'. Their syntax becomes peculiarly muddled, making their utterances so incomprehensible that we take them to be nonsensical. In the content of these utter-ances a connection to a bodily organ or innervation is often fore-grounded. To this we can add the fact that even in schizophrenic symptoms that resemble the substitute formations of hysteria and compulsion neurosis, the relationship between the repressed and its substitute displays peculiarities that we would find puzzling in either of those two neuroses.

Dr V. Tausk (Vienna) has made available to me some of his observations of the initial stages of a schizophrenia, which are par-ticularly valuable in that the patient herself sought to explain her own utterances. I shall illustrate the view I intend to advocate using two of his examples. I have no doubt, incidentally, that any observer could easily produce a wealth of such material.

One of Tausk's patients, a girl brought to the clinic after a quarrel with her lover, complains: *Her eyes are not right, they are twisted [verdreht]*. She herself explains this by producing, in coherent language, a series of reproaches against her lover. 'She just cannot understand him, he looks different every time, he is a hypocrite, a *deceiver [Augenverdreher*, literally: eye-twister], he has twisted her eyes, now she has twisted eyes, they are no longer her eyes, she sees the world with different eyes now.'

The patient's comments on her incomprehensible utterance amount to an analysis because they express the equivalent meaning in a generally comprehensible form; they simultaneously shed light on the meaning and genesis of schizophrenic word-formations. I agree with Tausk when, in this example, he highlights the fact that the association with an organ (the eye) has taken over representation of the whole thought content. Schizophrenic speech exhibits a hypochondriac trait here – it has become *organ language*.

A second statement from the same patient: 'She is standing in church, suddenly she feels a jerk, she *has to change her position, as if someone is positioning her, as if she is being positioned [gestellt]*.'

This was followed by the analysis in the form of a new series of reproaches against her lover, 'who is common, who has made her common, too, even though she was from a refined family. He has made her like himself by making her think he was better than her; now she has become the same as him, believing it would make her better if she was like him. He has *distorted* the truth about himself, now she is the same as him (identification!), he has *distorted [verstellt]* her'.

The movement of 'changing her position' [*Sich-anders-stellen*] is, Tausk points out, a representation both of the word 'distort' [*verstellen*] and of her identification with her lover. Again I would highlight the prevalence in this whole train of thought of that element which has as its content a physical innervation (or rather the sensation of one). A hysterical woman, incidentally, would in the first instance have convulsively twisted her eyes, and in the second have actually performed the jerking movement, instead of just feeling the impulse to do it or the sensation of it – and in neither instance would this have been accompanied by any conscious thoughts, nor would she have been able to express any in retrospect.

So far, these two observations testify to what we have called hypochondriac or organ language. But – more importantly, it seems – they also put us in mind of something else, which is illustrated again and again in, for example, the cases collected in Bleuler's monograph, something that can be expressed in a specific formula. In schizophrenia, *words* are subjected to the same process that turns latent dream-thoughts into dream images – we call it the *primary psychic process*. They become condensed together and transfer their whole investments to one another by means of displacement; the process can go so far that a single word, especially suitable due to its multiple connections, can come to represent a whole train of thought. Works by Bleuler, Jung and their pupils have provided a wealth of material that supports precisely this claim.[1]

Before we draw any conclusion from such observations, let us consider further the subtle, but none the less puzzling differences between the substitute formations in schizophrenia and those in hysteria and compulsion neurosis. A patient currently under my observation has withdrawn from all the interests of life on account of the poor state of his complexion. He claims to have blackheads and deep holes in his face that everybody notices. Analysis reveals that his castration complex is being played out on his skin. At first he occupied himself relentlessly with these blackheads; it gave him great pleasure to squeeze them because when he did so, something would spurt out, as he puts it. Then he began to believe that a deep pit had appeared wherever he had removed a blackhead, and he bitterly reproached himself for having permanently ruined his skin by 'constantly fiddling around with his hands'. For him, squeezing out the contents of a blackhead is evidently a substitute for masturbation. The holes that he is to blame for creating are female genitals, i.e., they represent the execution of the threat of castration (or the fantasy of this threat) provoked by his masturbation. Despite its hypochondriac character, this substitute formation is very similar to a hysterical conversion, and yet we get the feeling that something else must be going on here and that we could never put a substitute formation such as this down to hysteria, even before we can specify the actual basis of this difference. A hysteric would hardly adopt a tiny little cavity like a skin pore as a symbol for the vagina, which he will otherwise compare with every imaginable object containing a hollow space. We would also expect that the sheer number of these little cavities would prevent him from adopting them as a substitute for the female genitals. The same applies to the young patient about whom Tausk gave a report to the Viennese Psychoanalytical Society some years ago. In every other respect he behaved just like a compulsion neurotic, spending hours getting ready and so on. But the striking difference was that he was able to tell us what his inhibitions meant without any resistance. When putting on his socks, for example, he was disturbed by the idea that he would pull apart the stitches in the knitting – that is, the holes – and to him every hole was a symbol of the female genital opening. This, too, is something we would never expect from a compulsion neurotic; R. Reitler had one such neurotic under his observation who suffered from the same procrastination about putting his socks on; after his resistances were overcome, he found the explanation to be that his foot symbolized a penis, that putting a sock on represented a masturbatory act, and that he was compelled continually to put the sock on and take it off, partly to complete the representation of masturbation, partly to undo it.

If we ask ourselves what gives schizophrenic substitute formations and symptoms their strange character, we eventually realize it is the predominance of the word-relation over the thing-relation. As regards the thing itself, there is very little similarity between squeezing a blackhead and an ejaculation from the penis, and even less between the countless shallow pores on the skin and the vagina; but in the first instance something spurts out each time, and in the second the cynical saying 'a hole is a hole' quite literally holds true. The substitute is determined not by the similarity between two things, but by their identity when expressed in words. Where the two – word and thing – do not coincide, the process of schizophrenic substitute formation deviates from that in the transference neuroses.

In the light of this finding, we need to revise our assumption that object-investments are abandoned in schizophrenia by adding that the word-ideas of the object remain invested. What we were able to term the conscious object-idea can now be divided up into the *word-idea* and the *thing-idea*, the latter consisting in the investment, if not of direct memory-images of the thing, at least of more remote memory traces derived from these. All of a sudden we seem to realize what the difference is between a conscious and an unconscious idea. The two are not, as we supposed, different inscriptions of the same content at different psychic locations, nor are they functionally different states of investment at the same location; it is rather that the conscious idea comprises both the thing-idea and the corresponding word-idea, whereas the unconscious idea consists of the thing-idea alone. The *ucs* system contains the thing-investments of objects, the first and true object-investments; the *pcs* system comes into being when these thing-ideas are 'overinvested' by being linked with their corresponding word-ideas. We may suppose it is these over-investments that bring about a higher psychic organization and pave the way for primary processes to be superseded by the secondary processes that predominate in the *pcs*. We can also specify now what it is in the transference neuroses that repression actually withholds from the rejected idea, namely translation into words that are supposed to remain attached to the object. If an idea is not put into words, or if a psychic act is not overinvested, then it remains in the *ucs* in a state of repression.

I may point out just how early on we were in possession of this insight, which today enables us to understand one of the most striking characteristics of schizophrenia. In the final pages of *The Interpretation of Dreams*, published in 1900, I explain that thought processes, i.e., the acts of investment furthest removed from perceptions, are, in themselves, unconscious and without quality, and that they become capable of consciousness only through being linked with the perceptual traces of words. For their part, word-ideas also derive from sense perceptions just like thing-ideas, so we might wonder why object-ideas cannot become conscious by means of their own perceptual traces. But thought probably takes place in systems so far removed from the original perceptual traces that they have retained none of their qualities and need to be reinforced with new qualities in order for consciousness to be achieved. Besides, by being linked with words, investments can be endowed with qualities even when they have no perceptual qualities of their own because they represent only the relations between object-ideas. Relations such as these, which can be apprehended only through words, are a crucial element of our thought processes. We are aware that linking something with word-ideas does not amount to making it conscious, it merely makes this possible and is therefore characteristic only of the *pcs* system. Now, though, we see this discussion has led us away from our actual subject and into the thick of the problems of the preconscious and conscious, which, with good reason, we have reserved for a separate discussion.

With schizophrenia, which we are touching on here only in so far as seems indispensable for a general understanding of the *ucs*, the doubt must arise as to whether the process termed repression here still has anything at all in common with the repression in the transference neuroses. Our formula that repression is a process that occurs between the *ucs* and *pcs* (or *cs*) systems, resulting in something being kept away from consciousness, must in any case be revised if it is to include dementia praecox and other narcissistic disorders. Nevertheless, one common factor remains: attempted flight by the ego, manifesting itself in the withdrawal of the conscious investment. The briefest of reflections will tell us how much more thoroughly and radically this attempted flight, this flight of the ego is carried out in the narcissistic neuroses.

If, in schizophrenia, this flight consists in the withdrawal of the drive-investment from the areas representing the *unconscious* object-idea, it may seem strange that the element of this object-idea which belongs to the *pcs* system – the corresponding word-ideas – should, on the contrary, be invested more intensively. We might think it more likely that the word-idea, being the preconscious element, would have to bear the initial brunt of the repression, and that after the repression had progressed to the unconscious thing-ideas, the word-idea would be utterly incapable of investment. Admittedly, this is not easy to comprehend. It turns out that the investment of the word-idea has nothing to do with the act of repression, but instead represents the first of the attempts at recovery or cure that so conspicuously dominate the clinical picture of schizophrenia. These efforts are aimed at recovering lost objects, and it may well be to this end that they approach the object via its verbal element, but then have to content themselves with words instead of things. Our psychic activity in general proceeds in one of two opposing directions: either from the drives, through the *ucs* system towards conscious thought-activity, or from an external stimulus, through the *cs* and *pcs* systems towards the ego- and object-investments in the *ucs*. This second path must remain passable in spite of repression, and, to some extent, remains open to the efforts of the neurosis to recover its objects. When we think in abstract terms, we are in danger of neglecting the relations between words and unconscious thing-ideas, and it cannot be denied that our philosophizing thus begins to take on an unwelcome resemblance, both in expression and content, to the schizophrenic's approach. Conversely, we could attempt to characterize the schizophrenic mode of thought by saying they treat concrete things as if they were abstract.

If we have accurately identified what the *ucs* is and have correctly determined the difference between an unconscious and a preconscious idea, then our investigations in many different areas should lead us back to this same discovery.

(1915)

Note

1. Dream-work occasionally treats words like things, creating very similar 'schizophrenic' utterances or neologisms.

Negation

The manner in which our patients present their associations during analytical work gives us occasion for some interesting observations. 'Now you'll think I want to insult you, but I really don't mean to.' This, we realize, is a thought being rejected as it emerges, by means of projection. Or: 'You ask who this person in my dream can be. It's *not* my mother.' This we amend: 'So it is your mother.' In our interpretations we take the liberty of disregarding the negation and seizing on the pure content of the thought. It is as if the patient had said: 'My first thought was, it's my mother, but I have no desire to admit this.'

Occasionally we can get sought-after information about unconscious repressed material by a very easy method. We ask: 'So what would you say is absolutely least likely in this situation? What do you think was furthest from your mind at that point?' If the patient walks into the trap and tells us what he would find most incredible, he almost always gives the truth away. Compulsion neurotics who have already been initiated into an understanding of their symptoms often provide a nice counterpart to this experiment. They say: 'I've got a new compulsive idea. My immediate thought was, it could mean such and such. But no, surely that can't be true – otherwise I couldn't have had that thought.' The interpretation of the new compulsive idea that they reject with this argument picked up from the treatment is, of course, the correct one.

The content of a repressed idea or thought can get through to consciousness, then, on condition that it is *negated*. Negation is a way of acknowledging the repressed, indeed it amounts to a lifting of the repression, although not, of course, an acceptance of what is repressed. Here we see how an intellectual function differs from an emotional process. Only one of the consequences of the process of repression – that of the ideational content not being allowed into consciousness – is undone with the help of negation. The result is a kind of intellectual recognition of the repressed while the essential element of the repression remains in place.[1] During analytical work, we often produce a further very important and somewhat strange variant of this situation. We manage to overcome even the negation and bring about a full intellectual acknowledgement of the repressed – but still without lifting the repression itself.

Since it is the task of the intellectual function of judgement to affirm or negate the contents of thoughts, these remarks have led us to the psychological source of this function. To negate something in judgement is basically to say: 'This is something I'd rather repress.' Disapproval is the intellectual substitute for repression – its 'no' is a hallmark of repression, a kind of certificate of origin like 'Made in Germany'. By means of this symbol of negation, thought frees itself from the restrictions imposed by repression and appropriates material without which it could not perform its function.

Essentially, it is the function of judgement to make two kinds of decision. It has to decide whether or not a thing possesses a certain property, and whether or not an imagined thing exists in reality. The property to be decided on might originally have been good or bad, useful or harmful, or, expressed in the language of the most archaic, oral drive impulses: 'I want to eat this, or spit this out.' In more general terms: 'I want to take this into me, or keep it out of me,' that is: 'I want it inside me, or outside me.' As I have explained elsewhere, the primal pleasure-ego wants to introject into itself everything good and expel from itself everything bad. That which is bad, that which is alien to the ego, that which is outside, are initially identical as far as it is concerned.[2]

The other kind of decision that it is the function of judgement to make – whether or not an imagined thing exists in reality (reality-testing) – is a matter for the reality-ego, into which the primal pleasure-ego ultimately evolves. Now the question is no longer whether what is perceived (a thing) should be taken into the ego or not, but whether something already present in the ego, as a mental image, can also be rediscovered in perception (reality). We see that, once again, it is a question of *inside* and *outside*. That which is non-real, merely imagined, subjective, exists only on the *inside*; other things, real things, are also there on the *outside*. In this development, adherence to the pleasure principle has been set aside. Experience has taught that what matters is not only whether a thing (an object of satisfaction) possesses the property of 'goodness', and so merits being taken into the ego, but also whether it is actually there in the outside world, and so can be appropriated whenever the need arises. To understand this development, we have to remember that all mental images stem from – are reproductions of – perceptions. Originally, then, the mere existence of the idea of a thing is a guarantee that the thing actually exists. The opposition between subjective and objective does not exist from the start. It comes about only because thought has the capacity to bring back something once perceived by reproducing it as a mental image, with no need for the external object still to be present. The first and immediate aim of reality-testing, then, is not to discover, in real perception, an object corresponding to the mental image, but to *rediscover* it, to ascertain that it still exists. Another feature of the faculty of thought leads to a further widening of the gap between the subjective and the objective. The reproduction of a perception as a mental image is not always a faithful copy; it can be modified by omissions or by the fusion of various elements. Here the job of reality-testing is to assess the extent of these distortions. Clearly, though, what led to the actual inception of reality-testing was the loss of objects that had once brought real satisfaction.

Judging is the intellectual action which determines the choice of motor action, puts an end to pausing for thought, and leads the way from thought to action. I have discussed pausing for thought elsewhere, too. It should be regarded as a trial run of an action, a 'feeling out' involving a low expenditure of motor discharge. Now let us think: Where has the ego previously employed this kind of feeling out? Where did it learn the technique it now applies in thought processes? It was at the sensory end of the psychic apparatus, in connection with sense perceptions. Perception, according to our hypothesis, is not an entirely passive process, rather the ego periodically invests small amounts of energy in the perceptual system by means of which it samples the external stimuli, withdrawing again after each such exploratory advance.

Studying the phenomenon of judgement gives us perhaps our first insight into the way an intellectual function evolves from the play of primary drive impulses. Judging something is an expedient progression from the primal act, governed by the pleasure principle, of incorporating it into or expelling it from the ego. Its polarity seems to correspond to the opposition we have posited between two basic groups of drives. Affirmation – as a substitute for unification – belongs to Eros, negation – the successor to expulsion – belongs to the destruction drive. A general desire for negation, the negativism of some psychotics, can probably be regarded as indicating a drive disintegration caused by withdrawal of the libidinal components. But judgement is able to perform its function at all only because the creation of the symbol of negation provides thought with its first measure of independence from the effects of repression and so from the constraints of the pleasure principle.

Fully consonant with this view of negation is the fact that during analysis we never find a 'no' in the unconscious, and recognition of the unconscious by the ego is always expressed in negative formulations. There is no stronger evidence that the unconscious has successfully been uncovered than when the patient reacts with the words: *'That's not what I was thinking,'* or *'I wasn't thinking (have never thought) any such thing.'*

(1925)

Notes

1. This process is also the basis of the well-known phenomenon of 'tempting fate'. 'How nice that I haven't had one of my migraines for so long!' This, however, is the first sign of an attack, which we have already sensed approaching, but without wanting to believe it yet.
2. Cf. my comments in 'Drives and Their Fates'.

Fetishism

Over the last few years I have had the opportunity to study analytic-ally a number of men whose object choices were governed by a fetish. We need not suppose it was because of their fetish that these people came for analysis, for while its devotees recognize it as an abnormality, they rarely feel it to be the symptom of an illness; on the whole, they are perfectly happy with the fetish, and even extol the way it simplifies their love life. As a rule, then, their fetish came to light only incidentally during analysis.

The details of these cases cannot be published for obvious reasons. Nor, therefore, can I demonstrate the role played by accidental circumstances in the choice of fetish. The most remarkable case in this respect was one in which a young man had elevated a certain 'shine on the nose' into a fetishistic prerequisite. The surprising explanation for this was that the child had been brought up in England but had then come to Germany, where he almost com-pletely forgot his native language. The fetish, which stemmed from earliest infancy, needed to be read not in German, but in English; the 'shine [*Glanz*] on the nose' was actually a 'glance at the nose', so the fetish was the nose – which, incidentally, he could endow at will with this particular sheen, invisible to others.

What analysis revealed about the meaning and purpose of these fetishes was the same in every case. It emerged so spontaneously and seemed to me so compelling that I am prepared to anticipate the same general solution for all cases of fetishism. If I now state that a fetish is a penis substitute, this will no doubt come as a disappointment. I hasten to add, then, that it is a substitute not just for any penis, but for a specific and very special one, one which is of great significance in early infancy but which is subsequently lost. That is to say, it should normally be renounced, but it is precisely the purpose of a fetish to prevent this loss from occurring. To put it more plainly, a fetish is a substitute for the woman's (mother's) phallus, which the little boy once believed in and which – for reasons well known to us – he does not want to give up.[1]

What has happened, then, is this: the boy has refused to acknowledge the fact that he has perceived, that women have no penis. No, this cannot be true, because if women have been castrated, then his own penis is in danger, and the piece of narcissism, with which nature providently equips this very organ, recoils at the thought. In later life, an adult might experience a similar panic on hearing the cry that king and country are in peril, and it will have similarly illogical consequences. If I am not mistaken, Laforgue would say in this case that the boy 'scotomizes' his perception that women have no penis.[2] A new term is justified if it describes or highlights a new fact, but this is not the case here; the oldest piece of psychoanalytical terminology, the term 'repression', already refers to this pathological process. If, within this process, we wished to distinguish the fate of the idea more sharply from that of the emotion, and to reserve the term 'repression' for the emotion, then the correct term for the fate of the idea would be 'denial'. 'Scotomization' seems to me particularly unsuitable because it implies that the perception has been completely erased, with the same effect as if the visual impression had fallen on the retina's blind spot. On the contrary, though, our case reveals that the perception remains and a very energetic action has been undertaken to maintain the denial. It is not true that the child's belief in the female phallus remains unchanged after he has observed a woman. He both retains this belief and renounces it; in the conflict between the force of the unwelcome perception and the intensity of his aversion to it, a compromise is reached such as is possible only under the laws of unconscious thought, the primary processes. In his psyche, yes, the woman still has a penis, but this penis is no longer the same thing as before. Something else has taken its place, has been appointed its successor, so to speak, and this now inherits all the interest previously devoted to its predecessor. But because the horror of castration has been immortalized in the creation of this substitute, this interest also becomes intensified to an extraordinary degree. The repression that has taken place leaves behind a further *stigma indelebile* in the form of an aversion towards real female genitals, common to all fetishists. Now we have an overview of what the fetish achieves and how it is maintained. It remains a mark of triumph over the threat of castration and a safeguard against it; it also spares the fetishist from becoming homosexual, in that it endows women with a characteristic making them acceptable as sexual objects. In later life, the fetishist believes his genital substitute offers yet another advantage. Other people are unaware of its significance and so do not withhold it from him; the fetish is easily accessible and the sexual satisfaction it provides is readily available. What other men have to pursue and strive for presents no such problems for the fetishist.

Probably no male is spared the horror of castration at the sight of female genitals. Admittedly, we cannot explain why some men become homosexual as a result of this experience, others ward it off by creating a fetish, while the vast majority overcome it. It could be that, of all the various contributory factors, we do not know yet which ones determine the less common pathological outcomes; we shall just have to content ourselves with being able to explain what has happened, without, for the time being, worrying about explaining why something has not.

It seems reasonable to expect that the organs and objects chosen as substitutes for the missing female phallus will be those already used to symbolize the penis. This may well be the case often enough, but it certainly is not the decisive factor. The process involved when a fetish first becomes established seems reminiscent, rather, of the way memories are blocked out in traumatic amnesia. Here, too, the patient's interest stops in its tracks, so to speak, if indeed it is the last impression prior to the uncanny, traumatic one that becomes fixed as the fetish. Thus feet or shoes owe their prominence as fetishes, at least in part, to the fact that the curious boy looked at women's genitals from below, from the legs up; fur and velvet are – as we have long suspected – fixations on the sight of pubic hair, which should have been followed by the longed-for sight of the female member; pieces of underwear, so commonly adopted as fetishes, capture the moment of undressing, the last point at which the woman could still be regarded as phallic. But I do not wish to claim we know for certain how fetishes are determined in every case. I do, however, strongly recommend the study of fetishism to anyone who still doubts the existence of the castration complex, or anyone who can believe that dread of the female genitals has some other cause and derives from, say, a supposed memory of the trauma of birth. For me, however, the elucidation of fetishes held a further theoretical interest.

Recently I arrived, by pure speculation, at the formula that the essential difference between neurosis and psychosis was that in neurosis the ego, at the behest of reality, suppresses a piece of the id, whereas in psychosis it is impelled by the id to detach itself from a piece of reality; later I returned to this theme once again.[3] Soon afterwards, though, I had cause to regret having been so presumptuous. The analysis of two young men showed me that each of them, at the ages of two and ten respectively, had failed to acknowledge – 'scotomized' – the death of a beloved father, and yet neither had developed a psychosis. Here, then, a patently significant piece of reality had been denied by the ego, just as the fetishist denies the unwelcome fact of female castration. I also began to suspect that analogous occurrences are by no means uncommon in infancy, and I took this to be proof that my characterization of neurosis and psychosis was wrong. Of course, one possible way out remained open; my formula would just need to have been restricted to a more advanced level of differentiation in the psychic apparatus – the child was free to do something which, in an adult, would lead to serious harm. Further investigation, however, led to a different resolution of the contradiction.

As it turned out, the two young men had no more 'scotomized' their father's death than fetishists do female castration. Only one current in their psyche had failed to acknowledge the father's death; there was another that took full account of this fact. The wishful attitude and the realistic attitude existed side by side. In one of the cases, this split formed the basis of a moderately severe compulsion neurosis; in every situation in his life he would waver between two assumptions – one that his father was still alive and was holding him back from doing what he wanted, and the opposite one, that he had the right to consider himself his dead father's successor. Thus I can persist with my expectation that had this been a case of psychosis, one of these two currents – the realistic one – would actually be missing.

To return to my description of fetishism, let me say there are many further substantial pieces of evidence for the fetishist's dual attitude towards the issue of female castration. In particularly ingenious cases both the denial and affirmation of castration are incorporated within the structure of the fetish itself. This was the case with a man whose fetish consisted of a modesty girdle of the kind that can also be worn as a swimming costume. This piece of clothing completely concealed the genitals and the difference between them. According to analysis, it signified both that women were castrated and that they were not, and, furthermore, it allowed for the assumption of male castration, because all these possibilities could equally well be hidden beneath the girdle, the first incarnation of which, in infancy, had been a fig-leaf on a statue. A fetish such as this, doubly determined by an antithesis, naturally proves particularly resilient. In other cases the duality manifests itself in what the fetishist does with the fetish, either actually or in fantasy. To emphasize only that he worships the fetish does not tell the whole story; in many cases his treatment of it clearly amounts to an enactment of castration. Here, if he has developed a strong father-identification, he tends to adopt the role of the father, because it was to him that the child ascribed the act of castrating women. Affection and hostility towards the fetish, corresponding to the denial and acknowledgement of castration, combine in unequal proportions in each different case, so that one or the other is more clearly discernible. In this light, perhaps we can understand, albeit from a distance, the behaviour of men who like to cut off women's plaits and ponytails, where the need to act out the denied castration has pushed its way to the fore. This action fuses together the two incompatible beliefs – that women still have a penis, and that women have been castrated by the father. Another variant of – and ethno-psychological parallel to – fetishism may be seen in the Chinese custom of deforming women's feet and then revering the deformed foot as a fetish. It would seem Chinese men wish to show their gratitude towards women for having submitted to castration.

We can conclude by stating that the normal prototype of a fetish is the man's penis, just as the prototype of an inferior organ is the woman's actual little penis, the clitoris.

(1927)

Notes

1. This interpretation was published, without substantiation, as early as 1910 in my study *A Childhood Memory of Leonardo da Vinci*.

2. Let me correct myself, however, by adding that I have very good reason to believe Laforgue would say no such thing. We know from his own account that 'scotomization' is a term derived from the description of dementia praecox, not from any attempt to transfer psychoanalytical concepts to the psychoses, and that it is not applicable to processes of development or neurosis formation. He is very careful in his written account to make this incompatibility clear.

3. 'Neurosis and Psychosis' (1924) and 'The Loss of Reality in Neurosis and Psychosis' (1924).

The Splitting of the Ego in Defence Processes

I find myself for a moment in the interesting position of not knowing whether what I have to say should be regarded as something long known and self-evident or something completely new and strange. I suspect, however, it is the latter.

It has finally struck me that, in certain adverse situations, the youthful ego of the person we meet decades later as a patient in analysis must have behaved in a remarkable way. We could state in general – if rather vague – terms that the precondition for this behaviour is the influence of a psychic trauma. I would, however, prefer to focus on a clearly defined individual case, which, to be sure, will not cover every possible causal factor. Let us suppose the ego of the child finds itself governed by a powerful drive demand, which it is in the habit of satisfying; suddenly it has a terrifying experience which lets it know that to carry on satisfying the drive would lead to a real and almost intolerable danger. It now has to decide whether to acknowledge the real danger, submit to it, and refrain from satisfying the drive, or to deny reality, convince itself there is nothing to fear, and so hold on to the satisfaction. It is a conflict, then, between what the drive demands and what reality forbids. But the child does neither thing, or rather it does both simultaneously, which amounts to the same. It responds to the conflict with two contradictory reactions, each one valid and effective. On the one hand, with the help of certain mechanisms, it rejects reality and refuses any prohibition, on the other hand – and in the very same breath – it acknowledges the danger from reality, turns anxiety about it into a pathological symptom, and attempts subsequently to ward this anxiety off. We must admit this is a very neat solution to the problem. Each of the contending parties gets what it wants; the drive can go on being satisfied, and reality is accorded its due respect. But, as we all know, nothing in life is free except death. This success is achieved at the expense of a rift in the ego that will never heal, indeed it will widen as time goes on. The two contradictory reactions to this conflict persist as the focal point of a splitting of the ego. The whole process seems so strange to us because we take it for granted that ego processes tend towards synthesis. Evidently, though, we are wrong here. The – absolutely crucial – synthetic function of the ego has its own particular preconditions and is subject to a whole range of disorders.

Clearly it will be useful to insert the details of a specific case history into this schematic account. One boy became acquainted with female genitals through being seduced by an older girl when aged between three and four. When these relations were broken off, he kept this sexual stimulation going by means of enthusiastic manual masturbation, but he was soon caught by the vigilant nursemaid and threatened with castration, to be carried out, as usual, by the father. All the conditions were right, then, for a massive trauma. By itself, the threat of castration does not necessarily make much of an impression – the child refuses to believe it and can hardly even imagine the loss of such a highly valued part of his body. The sight of female genitals might have been enough to convince the boy in our case of this possibility, but at the time he had not made this deduction because his disinclination had been too strong and there had been no compelling reason to do so. On the contrary, he had silenced any stirrings of unease by declaring that what was missing had not appeared yet, she would grow one – a penis – later. Anyone with enough experience of small boys can remember some such remark being made at the sight of a little sister's genitals. When both factors coincide, however, it is a different matter. Now the memory of the perception, previously considered harmless, is revived by the threat and provides the dreaded corroboration of it. The boy now believed he understood why the girl's genitals were lacking a penis, and he no longer dared doubt that the same thing could happen to his own. From that moment on he had to believe castration was a very real danger.

The usual consequence of castration trauma, the one considered normal, is that the boy, either straight away or after something of a struggle, gives in to the threat with complete or at least partial obedience, in that he no longer touches his genitals. That is to say, he fully or partly renounces satisfaction of the drive. But we are prepared for our patient having found a different solution. He created a substitute for the woman's missing penis – a fetish. By so doing, he may have been denying reality, but he had safeguarded his penis. If he did not have to acknowledge that women had lost their penis, then the threat made against him lost its credibility, he no longer had to fear for his penis, and he could go on masturbating undisturbed. Our patient's action here seems like a clear case of turning away from reality, a process we would prefer to restrict to psychosis. Indeed, it is not very far removed from this, but let us reserve judgement, because closer analysis reveals a not insignificant distinction. The boy did not simply contradict his perception and hallucinate a penis where there was none, he merely carried out a displacement in value, transferring the significance of the penis to another part of the body, a process facilitated – in a way we need not explain here – by the mechanism of regression. Of course, this displacement related only to the female body; as far as his own penis was concerned, nothing had changed.

This – one might almost say crafty – way of dealing with reality determined how the boy behaved in practice. He carried on masturbating as if it involved no danger to his penis, but at the same time, in complete contrast to his apparent bravery or nonchalance, he developed a symptom that showed he had indeed acknowledged the danger. Immediately after having been threatened with castration at his father's hands, and simultaneously with his creation of a fetish, he developed an intense anxiety about being punished by his father. This was to become a lasting preoccupation for him, one he was able to overcome and overcompensate for only by bringing to bear the full force of his masculinity. Even this anxiety about his father bore no trace of anything to do with castration. With the help of regression to an oral phase, it manifested itself as an anxiety about being eaten by his father. It is impossible not to be reminded here of an archaic piece of Greek mythology, which tells how the old father-god Kronos swallowed his children and also wanted to devour his youngest son Zeus, and how Zeus, rescued by his mother's cunning, subsequently emasculated his father. To return to our case history, though, let me add that the patient produced a further, albeit minor symptom, which he retains to this day – an anxious sensitivity about his little toes being touched. It is as if, after all the to-ing and fro-ing between denial and acknowledgment, it was the castration that managed to find the clearer expression . . .

(1940 [1938])

PENGUIN MODERN CLASSICS

MASS PSYCHOLOGY AND OTHER WRITINGS
SIGMUND FREUD

Compulsive Actions and Religious Exercises / Mass Psychology and Analysis of
the 'I' / A Religious Experience / The Future of an Illusion / Moses the Man and
Monotheistic Religion / A Comment on Anti-Semitism

Translated by J. A. Underwood

With an Introduction by Jacqueline Rose

'Freud was an explorer of the mind ... an overturner and a re-mapper of accepted
or settled geographies and genealogies' Edward Said

These works reveal Freud at his most iconoclastic, asking challenging questions
about the powerful attraction of group identity and how this has the power to bind
us and drive us to hatred.

In *Mass Psychology* he explores the psyche as a social force, with a compelling
analysis of how institutions such as the Church and army can generate
unquestioning loyalty to a leader and provoke us to commit atrocities – Freud's
findings would prove all too prophetic in the years that followed. Works such as
'Moses the Man', written at the time of Freud's flight from Nazism in 1938, warn
of the dangers of nationalism. Writings like 'The Future of an Illusion' examine
religion and ritual in an unrelenting critique of religious faith.

General Editor: Adam Phillips

PENGUIN MODERN CLASSICS

BEYOND THE PLEASURE PRINCIPLE AND OTHER WRITINGS
SIGMUND FREUD

On the Introduction of Narcissism / Remembering, Repeating and Working Through / Beyond the Pleasure Principle / The Ego and the Id/Inhibition, Symptom and Fear

Translated by John Reddick

With an Introduction by Mark Edmundson

'Freud's great legacy ... brilliantly exposes the state of the psyche' Mark Edmundson

In Freud's view we are driven by the desire for pleasure, as well as by the desire to avoid pain. But the pursuit of pleasure has never been a simple thing. Pleasure can be a form of fear, a form of memory and a way of avoiding reality. Above all, as these essays show with remarkable eloquence, pleasure is a way in which we repeat ourselves.

The essays collected in this volume explore, in Freud's uniquely subtle and accessible style, the puzzles of pleasure and morality – the enigmas of human development.

General Editor: Adam Phillips

PENGUIN MODERN CLASSICS

STUDIES IN HYSTERIA
SIGMUND FREUD AND JOSEPH BREUER

Civilization and its Discontents / Civilized Sexual Morality and Modern Nervous Illness

Translated by Nicola Luckhurst

With an Introduction by Rachel Bowlby

'The effect that psychoanalysis has had upon the life of the West is incalculable'
Lionel Trilling

The tormenting of the body by the troubled mind – hysteria – is among the most pervasive of human disorders, yet at the same time it is the most elusive. Freud's recognition that hysteria stemmed from traumas in the patient's past transformed the way we think about sexuality.

Studies in Hysteria is one of the founding texts of psychoanalysis, revolutionizing our understanding of love, desire and the human psyche. As full of compassionate human interest as of scientific insight, these case histories are also remarkable, revelatory works of literature.

General Editor: Adam Phillips

PENGUIN MODERN CLASSICS

THE UNCONSCIOUS
SIGMUND FREUD

Formulations on the Two Principles of Psychic Functioning / Drives and their Fates / Repression / The Unconscious / Negation / Fetishism / The Splitting of the Ego in Defence Processes

Translated by Graham Frankland

With an Introduction by James Conant

One of Freud's central achievements was to demonstrate how unacceptable thoughts and feelings are repressed into the unconscious, from where they continue to exert a decisive influence over our lives.

This volume contains a key statement about evidence for the unconscious, and how it works, as well as major essays on all the fundamentals of mental functioning. Freud explores how we are torn between the pleasure principle and the reality principle, how we often find ways both to express and to deny what we most fear, and why certain men need fetishes for their sexual satisfaction. His study of our most basic drives, and how they are transformed, brilliantly illuminates the nature of sadism, masochism, exhibitionism and voyeurism.

General Editor: Adam Phillips

PENGUIN MODERN CLASSICS

THE PENGUIN FREUD READER
SIGMUND FREUD

Edited by Adam Phillips

'Freudian psychoanalysis changed the self-image of the western mind' Roy Porter

This major new collection brings together the key writings from every stage of
Freud's career to offer the perfect introduction to his life and work. Here are the
essential ideas of psychoanalytic theory, including Freud's explanations of such
concepts as the Id, Ego and Super-Ego, the Death Instinct and Pleasure Principle,
along with classic case studies like that of the Wolf Man.

Adam Phillips's marvellous selection provides an ideal overview of Freud's
thought in all its extraordinary ambition and variety. Psychoanalysis may be
known as the 'talking cure', yet it is also and profoundly a way of reading. Here
we can see Freud's writings as readings and listenings, deciphering the secrets of
the mind, finding words for desires that have never found expression. Much more
than this, however, *The Penguin Freud Reader* presents a compelling reading of
life as we experience it today, and a way in to the work of one of the most
haunting writers of the modern age.

PENGUIN MODERN CLASSICS

WILD ANALYSIS
SIGMUND FREUD

Translated by Alan Bance

With an Introduction by Adam Phillips

'These papers represent his most significant contributions to the subject over three decades' Adam Phillips

This powerful volume brings together Freud's major writings on psychoanalytic method and the question of psychoanalytic technique.

The fundamental concern of these works is the complex relationship between patient and analyst. Here Freud explores both the crucial importance of and the huge risks involved in patients' transference of their emotions on to their therapist. He also shows the ambiguous dangers of 'wild analysis' by doctors who are insufficiently trained or offer instant solutions; looks at issues such as the length of a treatment; and offers a trenchant discussion of the controversy surrounding psychoanalysis as a medical discipline. And, in examining the tensions between the practice of psychoanalysis and its central theory – the disruptive nature of the unconscious – Freud asks, can there ever really be rules for analysis?

General Editor: Adam Phillips

PENGUIN MODERN CLASSICS

THE UNCANNY
SIGMUND FREUD

Screen Memories / Leonardo da Vinci and a Memory of his Childhood / Family Romances / Creative Writers and Daydreaming / The Uncanny

Translated by David McLintock

With an Introduction by Hugh Haughton

'Freud ... ultimately did more for our understanding of art than any other writer since Aristotle' Lionel Trilling

Freud was fascinated by the mysteries of creativity and the imagination. The major pieces collected here explore the vivid but seemingly trivial childhood memories that often 'screen' far more uncomfortable desires; the links between literature and daydreaming – and our intensely mixed feelings about things we experience as 'uncanny'.

His insights into the roots of artistic expression in the triangular 'family romances' (of father, mother and infant) that so dominate our early lives, and the parallels between our own memories and desires and the tormented career of a genius like Leonardo, reveal the artistry of Freud's own writing.

General Editor: Adam Phillips

PENGUIN MODERN CLASSICS

AN OUTLINE OF PSYCHOANALYSIS
SIGMUND FREUD

New Introductory Lectures / An Outline of Psychoanalysis

Translated by Helena Ragg-Kirkby

With an Introduction by Malcolm Bowie

'Freudian psychoanalysis changed the self-image of the western mind' Roy Porter

No discovery has done more to shape modernity than Freud's theory of the unconscious and the part it plays in determining the course of our conscious lives. In psychoanalysis, Freud created a therapeutic tool by which the deepest anguish and desires of the psyche could be revealed.

Yet this vital and rewarding field has remained a mystery to many, and the widespread use of its terminology in everyday life can serve only to confuse matters further. *New Introductory Lectures* (1932) and *An Outline of Psychoanalysis* (1938) take us back to Freud's own account of his theories, and his wish to be the most lucid and inspiring advocate of psychoanalysis.

General Editor: Adam Phillips

PENGUIN MODERN CLASSICS

THE 'WOLFMAN' AND OTHER CASES
SIGMUND FREUD

'Little Hans' / The 'Ratman' / The 'Wolfman' / Some Character Types
Encountered in Psychoanalytic Work

Translated by Louise Adey Huish

With an Introduction by Gillian Beer

'Engrossing … Freud's narrative method gives a grandeur of scale to these
histories of ordinary lives' Gillian Beer

When a disturbed young Russian man came to Freud for treatment, the analysis of
his childhood neuroses – most notably a dream about wolves outside his bedroom
window – eventually revealed a deep-seated trauma. It took over four years to
treat him and 'The Wolfman' became Freud's most famous case.

This volume also contains the case history of five-year-old Little Hans's fear of
horses; the Ratman's violent fears of rats gnawing into his father and lover; and
the essay 'Some Character Types', in which Freud draws on the work of
Shakespeare, Ibsen and Nietzsche to demonstrate different kinds of resistance to
therapy. Above all, the case histories show us Freud at work, in his own words.

General Editor: Adam Phillips

PENGUIN MODERN CLASSICS

THE JOKE AND ITS RELATION TO THE UNCONSCIOUS
SIGMUND FREUD

Translated by Joyce Crick

With an Introduction by John Carey

'Daring ... brilliant and convincing' John Carey

Why do we laugh? The answer, argued Freud in this groundbreaking study of humour, is that jokes, like dreams, satisfy our unconscious desires.

The Joke and Its Relation to the Unconscious (1905) explains how jokes provide immense pleasure by releasing us from our inhibitions and allowing us to express sexual, aggressive, playful or cynical instincts that would otherwise remain hidden. In elaborating this theory, Freud brings together a rich collection of puns, witticisms, one-liners and anecdotes, many of which throw a vivid light on the society of early twentieth-century Vienna. Jokes, as Freud shows, are a method of giving ourselves away.

General Editor: Adam Phillips

Contemporary ... Provocative ... Outrageous ...
Prophetic ... Groundbreaking ... Funny ... Disturbing ...
Different ... Moving ... Revolutionary ... Inspiring ...
Subversive ... Life-changing ...

What makes a modern classic?

At Penguin Classics our mission has always been to make the best
books ever written available to everyone. And that also means
constantly redefining and refreshing exactly what makes a 'classic'.
That's where Modern Classics come in. Since 1961 they have been an
organic, ever-growing and ever-evolving list of books from the last
hundred (or so) years that we believe will continue to be read over and
over again.

They could be books that have inspired political dissent, such as
Animal Farm. Some, like *Lolita* or *A Clockwork Orange*, may have
caused shock and outrage. Many have led to great films, from *In Cold
Blood* to *One Flew Over the Cuckoo's Nest*. They have broken down
barriers – whether social, sexual, or, in the case of *Ulysses*, the
boundaries of language itself. And they might – like *Goldfinger* or
Scoop – just be pure classic escapism. Whatever the reason, Penguin
Modern Classics continue to inspire, entertain and enlighten millions
of readers everywhere.

'No publisher has had more influence on reading habits than Penguin'
Independent

'Penguins provided a crash course in world literature'
Guardian

The best books ever written

PENGUIN 🐧 CLASSICS

SINCE 1946

Find out more at www.penguinclassics.com